Human Rights Record of the United States in 2017

2017年美国的人权纪录

State Council Information Office of the People's Republic of China

中华人民共和国国务院新闻办公室

五洲传播出版社
China Intercontinental Press

图书在版编目（CIP）数据

2017年美国的人权纪录：汉英对照 / 中华人民共和国国务院新闻办公室编 .—北京：五洲传播出版社，2018.4
ISBN 978-7-5085-3568-5

Ⅰ . ① 2… Ⅱ . ①中… Ⅲ . ①人权 – 白皮书 – 美国 – 2017 – 汉、英
Ⅳ . ① D771.224

中国版本图书馆 CIP 数据核字（2018）第 074999 号

2017年美国的人权纪录

编　　者：国务院新闻办公室
出 版 人：荆孝敏
责任编辑：高　磊
制　　作：北京翰墨坊广告有限公司
出版发行：五洲传播出版社
地　　址：北京市海淀区北三环中路31号生产力大楼B座6层
邮　　编：100088
发行电话：010-82005927，010-82007837
网　　址：www.cicc.org.cn www.thatsbooks.com
印　　刷：北京圣彩虹科技有限公司
版　　次：2018年4月第1版第1次印刷
开　　本：889×1194mm　1/32
印　　张：3
字　　数：50千
定　　价：30.00元

Contents
目　录

Human Rights Record of the United States in 2017

State Council Information Office of the People's Republic of China

April 2018

Foreword

On April 20 local time, the State Department of the United States released its country reports on human rights practices for 2017, posing once again as "the guardian of human rights" and a self-styled "human rights judge." It continued to point fingers and cast groundless blame on the domestic affairs and human rights situation of other countries as if it had the most perfect human rights condition in the world. However, looking back on the year of 2017, even those with the slightest sense of righteousness will find that the human rights record of the United States itself remained tarnished and showed a continued deterioration tendency.

– On the evening of October 1, 2017, almost 60 people were killed and over 800 injured in a mass shooting in Las Vegas, the deadliest mass shooting in modern U.S. history.

– In August 2017, some white supremacists rallied in Charlottesville, chanting Nazi slogans in the "largest hate gathering in decades."

– According to reports on *The Atlantic* website and *New York Times* website, several polls of American scholars revealed that most of the respondents believed that quality of democracy in the United States had been plateauing for decades, and that American democracy is drowning in money.

– A research from Martin Gilens, a politics professor at Princeton University, showed that American economic policies over the last 40 years "strongly reflect the preferences of the most affluent, but bear virtually no relationship to the preferences of poor or middle-income Americans."

– A study from the U.S. National Registry of Exonerations released on March 7, 2017 showed that black Americans were about seven times more likely to be wrongfully convicted of murder than white Americans. When it comes to drug crimes, black Americans are about 12 times more likely to be wrongfully convicted than innocent white people. Black male offenders received sentences on average 19.1 percent longer than those of "similarly situated" white male offenders.

– The Economic Policy Institute released a report on February 13, 2017, saying that the average wealth for white families is seven times higher than average wealth for black families and that median white wealth is twelve times higher than median black wealth. More than one in four black households had zero or negative net worth.

– According to websites of *The Guardian* and the Office of the United Nations High Commissioner for Human Rights in December 2017, 52.3 million Americans lived in "economically distressed communities" and 18.5 million were living in deep poverty.

– A report of BBC on December 11, 2017 said that of those living in poverty in the United States, there were about 13.3 million children – 18 percent of those under the age of 18. The U.S. Urban Institute statistics revealed that nearly 9 million children in the United States (11.8 percent of American children) would grow up in persistently poor families.

I. Serious Infringement on Civil Rights

Violent crime was on the rise in the United States, the government exercised no effective control over guns which caused continuous growth of gun incidents, power abuse by American police sparked mass protests, and government surveillance infringed individual privacy. As a result, civil rights of the American people, especially the right to life and freedom, were seriously threatened.

Violent crime was on the rise in the United States. According to the FBI's annual report on national crime statistics released in September 2017, there were an estimated 1.2 million violent crimes in the United States in 2016, an increase of 4.1 percent from 2015. It showed the estimated rate of violent crime was 386.3 offenses per 100,000 inhabitants, up 3.4 percent compared with the 2015 rate. The estimated number of aggravated assaults, murders and rapes in the nation in 2016 increased 5.1 percent, 8.6 percent and 4.9 percent, respectively, when compared with the 2015 estimate (www.fbi.gov, ucr.fbi.gov, September 2017).

Ineffective gun control has caused continuous growth of gun violence in the United States. A Pew Research Center survey showed that at least two-thirds of the surveyed Americans had lived in a household with a gun at some point in their lives (www.pewsocialtrends.org, June 22, 2017). Seventy-three percent of the homicides for which the FBI received weapons data in 2016 involved the use of firearms, according to the FBI's annual report on national crime statistics released in September 2017 (www.ucr.fbi.gov, September 2017). According to the Gun Violence Archive of 2017, as of December 25, the total number of incidents in the United States was 60,091, which killed 15,182 and injured 30,619. Among the incidents, 338 were mass shooting (www.gunviolencearchive.org, December 25, 2017). On October 1, 2017, a gunman, named as 64-year-old Nevada resident Stephen Paddock, opened fire from the 32nd floor of the Mandalay Bay Hotel in Las Vegas towards an open-air music festival attended by 22,000. Nearly 60 people were killed and about 500 injured in the mass shooting, the deadliest in modern U.S. history (www.bbc.com, October 2, 2017). The police found 42 guns, thousands of bullets, and explosives in Paddock's hotel room and his home. On November 5, 2017, at least 26 were dead and 20 were injured after a man dressed in black entered First Baptist Church in Sutherland Springs, Texas armed with a rifle and opened fire on its congregation. Those shot ranged from 5 to 72 years old.

U.S. police abused their law enforcement power. According to statistics released by the FBI, law enforcement made an estimated 10,662,252 arrests nationwide in 2016. (Note: the UCR Program does not collect data on citations for traffic violations.) The arrest rate for the United States in 2016 was 3,298.5 arrests per 100,000 inhabitants (ucr.fbi.gov, September 2017). According to *The Washington Post*'s Fatal Force database, 987 people were shot by police in 2017. *The Washington Post* reported on July 26, 2017, that American police shot and killed a man while trying to serve a warrant at the wrong house. The man didn't have a warrant out for his arrest or a criminal record. Statistics released by Pew Research Center on January 11, 2017, showed that since 2015, almost 500 blacks had been fatally shot by police (www.pewsocialtrends.org, January 11, 2017). *Huffington Post* reported on November 7, 2017, that two American detectives Eddie Martins, 37, and Richard Hall, 33, were arrested on charges including raping a woman in a police van in New York after finding her in possession of marijuana and anti-anxiety pills.

Violent law enforcement by American police sparked mass protests in the United States. On February 22, 2017, hundreds of people took to the streets of Anaheim, Calif., for a sprawling protest that was sparked by video footage showing an off-duty Los Angeles police officer firing his gun during a confrontation with teenagers a day earlier. Police said they had arrested 23 people during the protests that followed (www.washingtonpost.com, February 23, 2017). Protesters in St. Louis on the night of September 15, 2017, blocked highways, damaged public and private property, broke windows, threw rocks at the mayor's house and threw bricks at police officers after a white former police officer earlier in the day was acquitted in the 2011 fatal shooting of a black man. Thirty-two protesters were arrested. "Time and time again, African-American men are killed by police, and nobody is held accountable," said one protester (abcnews.go.com, September 16, 2017).

Online surveillance by the U.S. government infringed individual privacy. According to a report by *Daily Mail* on April 6, 2017, Twitter refused a government demand to reveal who was behind an account opposed to President Donald Trump's tough immigration policies. The company filed a federal lawsuit to block the order, citing freedom of speech as a basis for not turning over records about the account. *The New York Times* reported on September 13, 2017, that there were nearly 15,000 forced searches of phones and laptops in the United States from October 2016 to March 2017, compared with 8,383 in the same period a year before. According to a report by *the Independent* on September 27, 2017, the American government quietly announced that it was planning on continuing to collect social media information on immigrants in America, a policy that has experts worried about privacy abuses and inefficiency. César Cuauhtémoc García Hernández, an associate professor of law at the University of Denver's Sturm College of Law, said that monitoring social media accounts could have a chilling effect on free speech. The U.S. Department of Justice was investigating protesters who exercised their First Amendment rights of free assembly at Donald Trump's inauguration in January 2017. The Justice Department has demanded the company DreamHost turn over some 1.3 million IP addresses of people who visited a website coordinating Inauguration Day protests (edition.cnn.com, August 17, 2017).

II. Systematic racial discrimination aggravates social split

The existing problems of racial discrimination in the United States have not been eased, but racial relations continue to worsen. Social antagonism has been intensified and racial conflicts frequently occurred.

Systematic racial discrimination exists in law enforcement and judicial organs. According to the website of *the Huffington Post* on November 18, 2017, a report of the U.S. Sentencing Commission released in November said that black male offenders received sentences on average of 19.1 percent longer than those of "similarly situated" white male offenders. According to the study from the National Registry of Exonerations, which was released on March 7, 2017, and examined cases from 1989 to October 2016, African Americans are far more likely to be wrongfully convicted of crimes such as murder, sexual assault and illegal drug activity than white people. Of the 1,900 defendants convicted of crimes and later exonerated, 47 percent were African Americans – three times their representation in the population (www.aljazeera.com, March 8, 2017). According to a report by the Stanford Open Policing Project released on June 19, 2017, based on analysis of more than 60 million police stops in 20 states, black and Latino drivers face a double standard and police require far less suspicion to search them than their white counterparts. Black and Latino drivers are about twice as likely to be searched compared with whites. After being stopped, black and Latino drivers are ticketed, searched and arrested more often than whites. For example, when pulled over for speeding, black drivers are 20 percent more likely than whites and Latino drivers 30 percent more likely than whites to be ticketed (www.latimes.com, June 19, 2017). According to statistics by the Mapping Police Violence released at its website on January 1, 2018, the U.S. police have killed 1,129 people in 2017, of whom 25 percent were black people, much higher than their population distribution of 13 percent.

According to a CNN report on September 1, 2017, a white police lieutenant Greg Abbott in the U.S. state of Georgia who has been an officer for more than 20 years stopped a white female driver. The woman said she was scared to move her hands and Abbott interrupted her and said, "You're not black. Remember, we only kill black people." On September 8, 2017, the AP reported that six black Philadelphia police officers filed complaints against their inspectors. Their complaints include referring to black civilians as "scum" and calling black civilian killings "thinning the herd."

Racist hate crimes hit record high in recent years. According to a new statistical report released by the Federal Bureau of Investigation (FBI) on November 13, 2017, a total of 6,121 hate crimes in the United States were reported to the FBI in 2016, to a point not seen in recent history. In the days after the November 2016 presidential election, an increase in racist slogans and hateful messages was reported, especially in schools. The Southern Poverty Law Center found 867 cases of hateful harassment or intimidation in the 10 days after the election (edition.cnn.com, November 13, 2017). According to a report by the website of Al Jazeera on June 10, 2017, white man Adam Purinton, 52, was accused of shouting "get out of my country" as he shot dead one Indian man and injured another at a bar in Kansas. According to the website of *New York Post* on October 31, 2017, in the summer of 2016, police arrested three men who smashed more than 40 headstones and spray-painted racial slurs and offensive phrases on many headstones that had Asian names on them at a Queens cemetery.

White nationalist protesters sparked violent confrontations. In August 2017, some white nationalists and right-wing protesters converged on Charlottesville, Virginia, shouting "blood and soil," a phrase invoking the Nazi philosophy (edition.cnn.com, August 12, 2017). White nationalist James Alex Fields Jr., 20, drove a car plowing into a group of protesters against white nationalists, killing one person and injuring 19 others (www.cbsnews.com, August 12, 2017). According to a report by *the Telegraph* on August 13, 2017, U.S. civil rights groups described the riot as America's "largest hate gathering in decades." On August 23, Anastasia Crickley, Chairperson of UN Committee on the Elimination of Racial Discrimination (CERD), said that "We are alarmed by the racist demonstrations, with overtly racist slogans, chants and salutes by white nationalists, neo-Nazis, and the Ku Klux Klan, promoting white supremacy and inciting racial discrimination and hatred." UN rights experts criticized U.S. government's failure to unequivocally reject racist violent events, and called on high-level politicians and public officials of the United States to unequivocally and unconditionally reject and condemn racist hate speech and crimes in Charlottesville and throughout the country (www.un.org, August 23, 2017).

Racial relations worsened. According to a Gallup poll released on March 15 last year, 42 percent of Americans say they personally worry a "great deal" about race relations in the United States, up seven percentage points from 2016 and a record high in Gallup's 17-year trend. This is the third straight year worries about this issue have increased by a significant margin. A survey, conducted by Pew Research Center in August, 2017, showed that 58 percent of Americans say racism is a "big problem in our society," up 8 percentage points in the past two years and having roughly doubled since 2011 (www.pewresearch.org, August 29, 2017). According to a report by BBC website on September 26, 2017, in 2016, National Football League (NFL) player Colin Kaepernick refused to stand up and kneeled during the national anthem. "I am not going to stand up to show pride in a flag for a country that oppresses black people and people of color," he said. A number of players have joined Colin Kaepernick since his demonstrations began.

Racial discrimination occurred frequently. According to a report by BBC website on May 31, 2017, NBA superstar LeBron James said that the "N-word" was spray painted on to his Los Angeles home. He said that racism will always be a part of America, and hate in America – especially for African-Americans – is living every day. *The New York Post* reported on September 15, 2017 that a volunteer firefighter in Ohio has posted racist remarks on Facebook, saying he'd save a dog from a burning house before a black man. "That's because one dog is more important than a million n——," he said. According to a report by the website of *New York Daily News* on November 3, 2017, two Asian school board candidates in central New Jersey received a racist attack. Residents in Edison received postcards that had photos of the two with "deport" stamped over their faces. Pew Research Center survey showed that some minority groups more frequently encounter harassment that carries racial overtones. A quarter of black Americans and ten percent of Hispanic Americans say they have been targeted online due to their race or ethnicity (www.pewresearch.org, July 25, 2017).

Minority groups have lower employment rate and are paid less. According to a report by the website of *Los Angeles Times* on September 15, 2017, since the Labor Department began keeping track of unemployment by race in the early 1970s, the black unemployment rate is nearly double the white unemployment rate. In 1979, the average black man in America earned 80 percent as much per hour as the average white man. By 2016, that shortfall had worsened to 70 percent, according to research from the San Francisco Fed (www.washingtonpost.com, September 5, 2017). A report by the website of *USA Today* on December 16, 2017, said that nationwide, the typical black household earns just 61 percent of the money that the typical white household earns. In Erie, Pennsylvania, the unemployment rate for white people is four percent, while that for black people is up to 24.6 percent. The median income for black people is only 43.2 percent of that for white people. A report by the website of *USA Today* on October 3, 2017, said that representation of all minority groups is declining in technology companies. According to a report released on March 29, 2017, by a San Francisco-based HR tech company, black people make up only two to three percent of the white-collar workforce – significantly less than their total workforce participation rate of 12 percent. Only about 5 percent of Hispanic workforce contributes to white-collar jobs (www.ibtimes.com, March 31, 2017).

Racial wealth gap becomes larger. According to data released by the Federal Reserve in September last year, between 2013 and 2016, wealth gap between black and white families grew by 16 percent during that time, and by 14 percent between Hispanics and whites. In 2016, white families had a median net worth of 171,000 U.S. dollars, compared with 17,600 U.S. dollars for blacks and 20,700 U.S. dollars for Hispanics, accounting for 10.29 percent and 12.11 percent of that for white families respectively (www.washingtonpost, September 28, 2017). The report issued by the Economic Policy Institute on February 13, 2017, said that more than one in four black households have zero or negative net worth (www.epi.org, February 13, 2017). The median income for an African American household was 39,490 U.S. dollars in 2016, according to U.S. Census Bureau data released in September 2017, even 1,873 U.S. dollars less than that in 2000. African Americans are the only racial group the Census Bureau identifies that has been left behind than the year of 2000 (www.latimes.com, September 15, 2017).

Muslims suffered from discrimination and assaults. On January 27, 2017, the U.S. government issued an order to ban on the entry of citizens from seven Muslim-majority countries: Iran, Iraq, Libya, Somalia, Sudan, Syria and Yemen. The order was labeled as "Muslim ban" as countries involved were mainly Muslim population, and aroused protests in the United States and the world. In a Pew Research Center survey conducted in early 2017, three-quarters of Muslim American adults say there is "a lot" of discrimination against Muslims in the United States, a view shared by 69 percent adults in the general public. In addition, half of U.S. Muslim adults say that in recent years it has become more difficult to be a Muslim in the United States. According to a Pew Research Center analysis of hate crimes statistics from the FBI, the number of assaults against Muslims in the United States rose significantly between 2015 and 2016, surpassing the modern peak reached in 2001, the year of the September 11 terrorist attacks (www.pewresearch.org, November 15, 2017).

III. Severe flaws in American-style democracy

Money politics in United States has gone further in 2017, as the wealthy groups controlled the political development; the disadvantaged groups faced more barriers in voting; and continuous scandals of political figures happened.

Money politics made inequality worse. *The Financial Times* website said on July 15, 2017 that the U.S. political system has been so warped by big money. According to Federal Election Commission data, dozens of political action committees collected tens of millions of dollars in the first season of 2017. Individual donors contributed 236.4 million U.S. dollars to political action committees and related political entities, roughly 30 percent more than the recorded contribution during the same span following the 2012 presidential election (www.bizjournals.com, May 8, 2017). The website of the Center for Responsive Politics on December 27, 2017, presented data which showed the lobbying spending in 2017 was the highest in the past five years (www.opensecrets.org, December 27, 2017). *The New York Times* website said in its commentary on September 20, 2017 that "American democracy is drowning in money." The money politics has made American economic policies over the last 40 years "strongly reflect the preferences of the most affluent, but bear virtually no relationship to the preferences of poor or middle-income Americans."

Democratic politics went weakening. An expert survey on American democracy showed that 89 percent of respondents believed the democratic quality in the United States had declined over the last 10 years (www.authwarningsurvey.com, June 28, 2017). *The Atlantic* website reported on June 21, 2017 that most interviewees of a survey on U.S. democracy disagreed that the U.S. met standards for granting citizens an equal opportunity to vote, stopping officials from exploiting their public office for private gain, and conducting politics and formulating policy.

Low-income voters faced more severe barriers. A report on November 21, 2017 from the website of *Newsweek* magazine said that hundreds of thousands of Americans were being denied the right to vote because they are poor. In nine states, legislators have enacted laws that disenfranchise anyone with outstanding legal fees or court fines. In Alabama, more than 100,000 people who owe money – roughly 3 percent of the state's voting-age population – have been struck from voting rolls. The report commented that preventing people from voting because they owe legal fees or court fines muzzle low-income Americans at a time in the nation's history when the rich have more political power than ever.

Older and physically challenged voters encountered more barriers. *The New York Times* website reported on November 24, 2017 that voting machines at polling places made it difficult for the elderly and disabled citizens of any age to vote. A survey of 178 polling places showed that the great majority still had impediments outside – like steep ramps or inadequate parking – or inside that could discourage or exclude disabled voters.

The media was suppressed. In 2017, a number of news organizations were rejected by the U.S. government in press conferences and other official activities and the CNN, *New York Times*, and other media organizations were barred from White House briefings. Press freedom in the United States is at its lowest point in 13 years, according to a report in 2017 (www.cnn.com, April 28, 2017). Another survey from the Pew Research Center on April 4, 2017 showed that 73 percent of adult respondents believed the tensions between the government and the news media were getting in the way of access to important national political news and information (www.journalism.org, April 4, 2017).

Corruption scandals broke out. A survey in 2017 showed that nearly six in 10 Americans believed the level of government corruption has risen in 2017, and nearly seven in 10 people said the government was doing a bad job at combating corruption. The website of CBS News reported on March 14, 2017 that nine military officers including the retired Navy admiral Bruce Loveless were indicted in a bribery scandal as they accepted the services of prostitutes, lavish meals and fancy trips from a defense contractor. The case has charged more than 20 former or current Navy officials.

Sexual scandals of congressmen continue to happen. *The USA Today* website said on November 20, 2017 that since 2016 at least 40 lawmakers in 20 states have been publicly accused by more than 100 people of some form of sexual misconduct or harassment. The website of Al Jazeera reported on December 12, 2017 that Democratic Congressman Al Franken, and others have faced the allegations of sexual harassment. According to a report on *the Washington Post* website on December 21, 2017, a senator's office used Treasury Department fund to settle a claim of sex discrimination or harassment, and the House of Representatives said its member-led offices were involved in settlements of at least 10 allegations of sexual harassment or sex discrimination since 2008. Another report also from *the Washington Post* website on December 1, 2017 said that the allegations against several political figures were being shielded by their parties, showing an ugly portrait of American politics.

IV. Rich-Poor Divide Continues Widening

The rich-poor divide expanded in the United States, reporting an increasing number of homeless people. Drugs and banned substances were abused, and people in poverty lived in miserable conditions. "The American Dream is rapidly becoming the American Illusion," said the independent human rights expert appointed by the UN Human Rights Council to look at poverty and human rights in countries around the world (www.theguardian.com, December 15, 2017).

The conditions remained precarious for people living in poverty. *The Guardian* news website reported on December 8, 2017 that 52.3 million Americans lived in "economically distressed communities," representing 17 percent of the U.S. population (www.theguardian.com, December 8, 2017). The most recent official statistics from the US Census Bureau indicated that more than 40 million people were living in poverty. Almost half of those, 18.5 million, were living in deep poverty, with reported family income below half of the poverty threshold (www.ohchr.org, December 15, 2017). According to a 2017 report issued by Stanford Center on Poverty and Inequality, the overall poverty rate in the United States' rural South stood at 20 percent, with blacks and black women in the rural South facing poverty rates of 33 percent and 37 percent, respectively. Native Americans in the rural West had the poverty rate as high as 32 percent (inequality.stanford.edu). After his two-week visit in the United States, Philip Alston, the United Nation's special rapporteur on extreme poverty and human rights stated that the United States is one of the word's richest and most powerful and technologically innovative countries; but neither its wealth nor its power nor its technology is being harnessed to address the situation in which 40 million people continue to live in poverty. The conclusion he drew was that "the persistence of extreme poverty is a political choice made by those in power" (www.theguardian.com, December 15, 2017).

Inequality deteriorated. The wealth gap continued to widen in the United States. According to the World Income Inequality Database, the United States has the highest Gini coefficient (measuring inequality) of all Western Countries. In the OECD, the United States ranks 35th out of 37 in terms of poverty and inequality (www.theguardian.com, December 15, 2017). In a report showing the share of U.S. household wealth by income level, Deutsche Bank's chief international economist Torsten Slok said the top 0.1 percent of American households hold about the same amount of wealth as the bottom 90 percent (www.

businessinsider.com, January 25, 2017). *Boston Review*'s website reported on Sept. 1, 2017 that while the income of those in the bottom 80 percent of America has grown only by about 25 percent in the last four decades, it has almost doubled for the top 20 percent. The United Nations monitor on poverty and human rights accused the U.S. leadership of attempting to turn the country into the "world champion of extreme inequality" (www.theguardian.com, December 15, 2017).

The life of the homeless was miserable. *The Guardian*'s website reported on December 6, 2017 that 553,742 people were homeless on a single night in the United States last year, with an increase of 4.1 percent in New York. In a homeless encampment in Los Angeles, approximately 1,800 homeless people shared just nine toilets located in stalls without doors at night (www.theguardian.com, June 30, 2017). Matthew Desmond's book Evicted said millions of Americans were evicted each year as they struggled to make rent: these people were the true forgotten poor (www.theguardian.com, February 24, 2017).

The U.S. government failed in controlling drug and addictive medicine. The website of *Medical Press* reported on June 13, 2017 that 7.7 million Americans abused illicit drugs. On December 14, 2017, CNN said nearly 40 percent of 12th-graders, 28 percent of 10th-graders and 12.9 percent of eighth-graders had used some sort of illicit drugs in the past year. CBS News reported on June 6, 2017 on its website that between 2011 and 2015, nearly four billion opioid pills were prescribed in the state of Ohio alone. Overdoses are now the leading cause of death of Americans under the age of 50. According to a report from the U.S. Centers for Disease Control and Prevention in December, 2017, in 2016, there were more than 63,600 drug overdose deaths in the United States. On December 12, 2017, ABC News reported that soaring use of opioids had forced tens of thousands of children to leave their homes across the United States, citing a 32 percent spike in drug-related foster care cases from 2012 to 2016.

The health care system was deeply flawed. Philip Alston, the UN's special rapporteur on extreme poverty and human rights, observed in a report that the "health gap" between the United States and its peer countries continued to grow and that Americans could expect to live shorter and sicker lives. Medical expenses and health insurance costs kept rising, with drug prices for chronic illnesses from asthma to cancer hitting record highs in the United States, *The Guardian* reported on its website on December 15, 2017 (www.theguardian.com, December 15, 2017). Results of a survey released by Pew Research Center on December 14, 2017 showed positive ratings for the government's handling of ensuring access to health care had declined 20 percentage points since 2015 (www.people-press.org, December 14, 2017).

V. Special Groups Suffer Discrimination and Physical Assault

American women faced obvious discrimination on employment and career development. The poverty, health and safety problems of children were worrisome. Persons with disabilities suffered from violent victimization. Rampant sex harassment and infringement contributed to a swarm of protests.

– Women suffered from serious threats of sex harassment and infringement. In October 2017, the scandal of American film producer Harvey Weinstein who sexually harassed a number of female stars broke out. Many Americans from all walks of life initiated a "#MeToo (Victim)" campaign on social media platforms to encourage the victims to protest against the widespread sex harassment and infringement, receiving active responses from about a million people. According to a report from the U.S. Equal Employment Opportunity Commission, 60 percent of women experienced harassment at work (https://www.usatoday.com, December 8, 2017). According to a report published on November 22 in 2017 on BBC website, former USA Olympic gymnastics sports doctor Larry Nassar was charged with sexual assault against more than 130 women in his care, including a number of Olympic gold medalists. According to a report published on December 18 in 2017 on the website of *Huffington Post*, Alex Kozinski, a federal appeals court judge, received accusations from multiple former female clerks of inappropriate sexual behavior. According to the annual sex harassment report published in May 2017 by the U.S. Department of Defense, 14,900 cases of sex harassment happened in 2016 in the army (http://abc7ny.com, December 13, 2017). According to a report published on December 15 in 2017 on the website of *Huffington Post*, the privacy of the female victims could not be guaranteed and they lived in fear that people were going to track them down and figured out who they were, which inflicted negative impact on the victims to lodge a sex harassment accusation.

– Serious gender discrimination on employment and career development. According to an employment report from the U.S. Bureau of Labor Statistics, the retail trade lost 54,300 jobs between October 2016 and October 2017, but the experiences between men and women were starkly different: women lost 160,300 jobs, while men gained 106,000 jobs (http://iwpr.org). According to a Pew Research Center survey, 57 percent of women say the country hasn't done enough to give women equal rights with men and 38 percent of women cite gender discrimination experiences related to hiring, pay or promotion (http://www.pewsocialtrends.org).

– Children's personal rights faced serious threats. According to statistics released in July 2017 by the FBI, 68,068 cases of physical assault against children aged less than 10 years old were reported in the United States in 2016, 97,588 such cases against children aged between 11 and 15 years old and 159,963 such cases against youths aged between 16 and 20 years old. Among all the cases, 83,611 are sex offense cases (http://ucr.fbi.gov). According to a report released on November 28 in 2017 by the U.S. Institute for Women's Policy Research, nearly one in five high school girls experienced bullying while over a quarter of Hawaii women reported unwanted sexual contact in their lifetime.

– The health condition of poor children was worrisome. According to a BBC report on December 11 in 2017, there were

13.3 million poor children out of the U.S. poverty-stricken population, accounting for 18 percent of U.S. children. Nearly 9 million children in the United States (11.8 percent) were grown up in persistently poor families, accounting for 11.8 percent of the U.S. children (http://www.mobilitypartnership.org, May 18, 2017). According to a survey on the health condition of the public housing residents in the District of Columbia, 33 percent of adult interviewees reported having a child with asthma, 21 percent of them reported having an overweight child and 14 percent of them reported having a child with a chronic disease (http://www.mobilitypartnership.org, March 6, 2017).

– Violent victimization against persons with disabilities. According to statistics released in July 2017 by the U.S. Bureau of Justice Statistics, the rate of violent victimization against persons with disabilities was 2.5 times higher than that for persons without disabilities above 12 years old between 2009 and 2015. The rate of violent crimes against persons with disabilities tripled that for persons without disabilities (http://www.bjs.gov). According to statistics from the 2016 FBI Hate Crime Statistics Program released in 2017, out of the 6,063 single-bias incidents reported in 2016, 1.2 percent of them were prompted by disability bias (http://ucr.fbi.gov).

VI. Continued Violations of Human Rights in Other Countries

The US-led military operations in other countries have caused heavy civilian casualties. The Guantanamo Bay detention camp continued to detain and torture foreigners. The United States also made cyber warfare tools, hacking and spying foreign networks.

War of aggression on Syria caused a large number of civilian casualties. On June 19, 2017, *The New York Times* website reported that the U.S. administration had given the military "total authorization" to decide how, and how much, force would be used, while the American military had relaxed the oversight, investigation and accountability on civilian casualties, resulting in the civilian death toll ticking upward. The US-led coalition and Marines had bombed or shelled at least 12 schools, 15 mosques, 15 bridges as well as residential neighborhoods, hospitals, cultural relics and refugee camp. The coalition warplanes also launched a barrage of airstrikes targeting the boats, on which many families waited to cross a river to escape, reportedly massacring as many as 21 civilians (www.motherjones.com, August 6, 2017). *The Muslim Times* website reported on June 24, 2017 that the US military had attacked Syrian government forces "at least four times in recent months," including a missile strike in April against a Syrian airfield. Myles Hoenig, an American political analyst, said the United States was violating the UN Charter by conducting a war of aggression against Syria (muslimtimes.co, June 24, 2017).

Foreigners have long been tortured and detained at the Guantanamo Bay. On December 13, 2017, The American Broadcasting Company website reported that the new U.S. administration had not released any prisoners from the Guantanamo Bay and not added any to the list of cleared men who can go home, or to a third country, for resettlement. The Al Jazeera website reported on September 22, 2017, that in a hearing of the Inter-American Commission on Human Rights (the Commission), former Guantanamo detainee Djamel Ameziane prepared a written statement saying he was detained for 11 years, faced prolonged incommunicado detention, multiple forms of torture, and never received a judicial determination regarding the legality of his detention. According to a report of *The USA Today* website on December 13, 2017, the U.N. and human rights organizations had criticized U.S. authorities for creating a "legal black hole" allowing for the infinite detention of suspects without charge, and for holding many of the detainees for more than a decade. Nils Melzer, the United Nations Human Rights Council special rapporteur on torture, on December 13, 2017, urged the United States to end its torture of detainees held at the controversial Guantanamo Bay detention facility (www.usatoday.com, December 13, 2017).

Making cyber warfare tools. The US National Security Agency (NSA) operators had hacked into Pakistani mobile networks and had been spying on hundreds of IP addresses in the country, WikiLeaks claimed (economictimes.indiatimes.com, April 11, 2017). On May 14, 2017, the Zero Hedge website revealed that NSA created "Top Secret Arsenal" of tools that allowed anyone to "back door" into virtually any computer system. An unknown group of hackers used the same set of NSA-created tools to launch a global malware cyber attack by using ransomeware virus, holding at least 200,000 computer systems around the globe hostage (www.zerohedge.com, May 14, 2017).

Chronology of Human Rights Violations of the United States in 2017

JANUARY

January 6

The AP website reported that an army veteran drew a gun from his checked luggage on arrival at the Fort Lauderdale airport and opened fire, killing five people and wounding eight.

January 11

The Pew Research Center revealed that since 2015, almost 500 blacks have been fatally shot by police. Their deaths and the disputed circumstances surrounding many of these incidents have sparked widespread protests over police tactics.

January 27

The U.S. administration signed an executive order saying that it was necessary to suspend for at least four months the resettlement of refugees from around the world – and those from Syria indefinitely; and for at least 90 days block entry of visa holders from Iran, Iraq, Libya, Somalia, Sudan, Syria and Yemen.

January 28

Protests broke out in many cities around the United States against the White House order suspending the entry of refugees and others from several majority-Muslim nations.

January 31

The USA Today website reported that referring to the order as a "Muslim Exclusion Order," 27 plaintiffs from across the US filed a lawsuit and complained that the order "implements an impermissible religious gerrymander that divides foreign nationals, even those lawfully present inside the United States, into favored and disfavored groups based on their faith."

FEBRUARY

February 13

The U.S. Economic Policy Institute released a report saying that average wealth for white families was seven times higher than average wealth for black families. Median white wealth was twelve times higher than median black wealth. More than one in four black households have zero or negative net worth, compared to less than one in ten white families without wealth.

February 21

The Forbes website reported that student loan debt was the second highest consumer debt category – higher than both credit cards and auto loans. There were more than 44 million borrowers with 1.3 trillion dollars in student loan debt in the United States alone. The average student in the Class of 2016 had 37,172 dollars in student loan debt.

February 22

The CNN website reported that a total of 214 people have been indicted since January 20 on felony rioting charges in connection with the Inauguration Day protests in downtown Washington.

February 23

The Washington Post website reported that on the evening of February 22, hundreds of people took to the streets of Anaheim, Calif. for a protest against an off-duty Los Angeles police officer firing his gun during a confrontation with teenagers a day earlier. A total of 23 people were arrested during the protest.

February 24

The Guardian website reported that one of the first things the new U.S. administration did was to make a huge number of middle-income families considerably worse off. Just hours after the inauguration it reversed the previous administration's decision to cut Federal Housing Administration insurance premiums by 0.25 percent. Millions of Americans are evicted each year as they struggle to make rent: these people are the true forgotten poor.

MARCH

March 6

The website of the Urban Institute reported that 33 percent of households in public housing have a member aged 62 or older and 39 percent have children, while 21 percent of residents have a disability. In a report on health condition of people in public housing in the District of Columbia, 33 percent of the surveyed adults reported having a child with asthma, 21 percent reported having an overweight child, and 14 percent reported having a child with a chronic health condition.

March 7

The National Registry of Exonerations reported that African Americans are far more likely to be wrongfully convicted of crimes such as murder, sexual assault and illegal drug activity than white people, according to a review of exonerations from 1989 to October 2016. Of the 1,900 defendants convicted of crimes and later exonerated, 47 percent were African Americans – three times their representation in the population.

March 14

The CBS website reported that a retired Navy admiral is among nine military officers who have been indicted in a burgeoning bribery scandal. Retired Adm. Bruce Loveless and the other officers accepted the services of prostitutes, lavish meals and fancy trips from a businessman in exchange for helping his company. The indictment has charged more than 20 former or current Navy officials so far.

March 15

The Gallup issued a poll showing that 42 percent of Americans say they personally worry a "great deal" about race relations in the United States, up seven percentage points from 2016 and a record high in Gallup's 17-year trend. This is the third straight year worries about this issue have increased by a significant margin.

On the same day, the website of the Institute for Policy Studies reported that Wall Street banks handed out 23.9 billion U.S. dollars in bonuses to 177,000 New York City-based employees in 2016, which were 1.6 times the combined annual earnings of all 1,075,000 U.S. full-time minimum wage workers. Since 1985, the nominal value of the average Wall Street bonus has increased 890 percent, whereas the minimum wage has risen only 116 percent.

March 28

The Washington Post website reported that the U.S. Congress proposed to wipe away landmark online privacy protections, a significant reworking of the rules governing Internet access. If the legislation is approved, providers will be able to monitor their customers' behavior online and, without their permission, use their personal and financial information to sell highly targeted ads. "It means that Americans will never be safe online from having their most personal details stealthily scrutinized and sold to the highest bidder," said Jeffrey Chester, executive director of the Center for Digital Democracy. It is "a tremendous setback for America."

APRIL

April 4

A *USA Today* website report quoted statistics from the Institute for Women's Policy Research as saying that women overall earned about 82% of the full-time weekly pay check of a man. Black women's earnings were just 68% compared to white men and Hispanic women's were 62%.

April 6

The Daily Mail website reported that Twitter had received an administrative summons in March demanding it to reveal who is behind an account opposed to the U.S. President's tough immigration policies. The government gave no reason for the demand. Twitter said the summons was an abuse of law.

April 11

A report on *the Economic Times* website quoted WikiLeaks as saying that the U.S. National Security Agency operators have hacked into Pakistani mobile networks and have been spying on hundreds of IP addresses in the country.

April 11

The Washington Post website reported that a passenger was forcibly dragged off an overbooked United Airlines plane. The passenger, bleeding, appeared to be of Asian origin and was overheard complaining that this might have been a factor in his treatment.

April 30

Website of *the Independent* reported that the Pentagon said at least 352 civilians have been killed in the US-led strikes in Iraq and Syria since operations began in 2014. Transparency project Airwars claimed that over 3,000 civilians have been killed in the bombing campaign.

MAY

May 8

According to the Federal Election Commission data, dozens of political action committees collected tens of millions of dollars in the first three months of 2017. Individual donors contributed 236.4 million U.S. dollars to political action committees and related political entities during the quarter, 30 percent more than contributions recorded during the same period following the 2012 presidential election.

May 11

Rane Baldwin, an African American woman, booked two First-Class American Airlines tickets from Kentucky to North Carolina on May 2 with her white friend, but she was told after boarding that the plane had fewer First Class seats than originally thought, *The Sun* website reported. Her seat had been changed to a row in the back of the plane while her white friend stayed in First Class.

May 11

According to data released on May 10 by the U.S. Census Bureau, an estimated 61.4 percent of Americans who were qualified to vote cast ballots in the 2016 presidential election, dipping to the lowest rate in 16 years, *The Hill* website reported. Only 49 percent of Asian Americans and 47.6 percent of Hispanic Americans turned out to vote; voter turnout among black voters fell almost seven percentage points from 2012 to 59.4 percent.

May 14

The Zero Hedge website reported that a group of hackers used the U.S. National Security Agency's "Top Secret Arsenal" of tools, which allow anyone to "back door" into virtually any computer system, to create the ransomware virus and launch a global malware cyberattack, holding at least 200,000 computer systems around the globe hostage.

May 15

According to data released by the U.S. Census Bureau, there were 245.5 million Americans aged 18 and older in November 2016, about 157.6 million of whom were registered to vote, the Pew Research Center website reported. By international standards, only 55.7 percent of the U.S. voting-age population cast ballots in the 2016 presidential election, putting the US behind most member states of the Organization for Economic Cooperation and Development.

May 17

According to the website of U.S. Equal Employment Opportunity Commission, Carolina Creek company demoted employee Korrie Reed after learning she had a pregnancy-related complication. This violated federal anti-discrimination laws. After Reed told the company's executive director that she believed her demotion was illegal, Carolina Creek fired her and then sued her in two different lawsuits.

May 31

The BBC website reported, an "N-word" was spray painted on to NBA superstar LeBron James' Los Angeles home. He said, "No matter how much money you have, no matter how famous you are… being black in America is tough." "Racism will always be a part of America, and hate in America – especially for African Americans – is living every day."

JUNE

June 1

U.S. President Donald Trump announced that the country would step away from the climate change agreement signed in 2015 in Paris, *the Washington Post* website reported. The article commented that the decision makes little sense since climate change is a real threat to Americans' health. However, the government viewed this international agreement solely through the lens of economic benefits to the United States.

June 9

CNN reported that William Boucher, a 23-year-old white man in Chicago, spitted at a black man for no reason, telling him that his children are "disposable vermin" and calling a second black man a slave.

June 10

Al Jazeera website reported that Adam Purinton, a 52-year-old white man, shouted "get out of my country" as he shot dead one Indian man and injured another at a bar in Kansas.

June 21

In a poll of more than 1,000 political scientists in the United States, most respondents believed that American democracy had been plateauing for decades and that the U.S. government failed to meet democratic standards for granting citizens an equal opportunity to vote or stopping officials from exploiting their public office for private gain, *The Atlantic* website reported.

June 22

The San Diego Union Tribune website reported that disability advocacy organization ADAPT organized a demonstration to protest against cutting Medicaid funding. Bruce Darling, an organizer, wrote in a statement that the American Health Care Act caps and significantly cuts Medicaid which will greatly reduce access to basic medical services for elderly and disabled Americans who rely on them.

June 30

Latest statistics show Los Angeles County saw a 23 percent increase in the number of homeless people, to 57,794, *The Guardian* website reported. For the approximately 1,800 people sleeping on the surrounding streets of Los Angeles' Skid Row, only nine cisterns without doors are available at night.

JULY

July 5

The Financial Times website reported that "in reality the US political system has been so warped by big money that it is now effectively controlled by an elite Republican oligarchy answerable primarily to ultra-rich donors that has succeeded by gerrymandering and other nefarious acts to create a situation where, even if it does not control all branches of government, it will still be well positioned to block any agenda seeking to change the status quo."

July 11

A new Pew Research Center survey finds that about 67 percent of 18-to 29-year-olds have experienced some form of online harassment, with young women the most likely to face online abuse. About 21 percent of women aged between 18 and 29 say they have been sexually harassed online, and 53 percent of them say they have been sent explicit images that they didn't ask for.

July 22

The Intercept.com website reported that the US was re-escalating its war in Afghanistan, expanding its operations in Iraq and Syria, conducting covert raids in Somalia and Yemen.

July 22

The Independent website reported that an errant U.S. air strike in July 21 killed 16 Afghan National Police officers who were fighting the Taliban and wounded two others.

July 25

A Pew Research Center survey finds that American minority groups more frequently encounter online harassment that carries racial overtones. A quarter of black Americans say they have been targeted online due to their race or ethnicity. Some 74 percent of blacks and 72 percent of Hispanics consider online harassment to be a "major problem," while 68 percent of blacks are more likely to say it is more important for people to feel safe and welcome online than to be able to speak their minds freely.

July 26

The Washington Post reported that two policemen went to a wrong address and shot dead an innocent person when executing an arrest warrant. The victim had no crime records.

AUGUST

August 5

The Guardian website reported that according to statistics from the International Organization for Migration, 232 people attempting to cross the U.S. border from Mexico died in first seven months of 2017, up 17 percent year on year.

August 6

The Mother Jones website reported that the US-led coalition's use of white phosphorus munitions on the outskirts of al-Raqqa, Syria, was unlawful and might amount to a war crime.

August 12

CNN reported that some white nationalists and right-wing protesters converged on Charlottesville, shouting "blood and soil," a phrase invoking the Nazi philosophy of "Blut und Boden."

August 12

The CBS website reported that James Alex Fields Jr., a 20-year-old white nationalist, drove a car that plowed into a group of counter-protesters, killing one person and injuring 19 others.

August 13

The Telegraph website reported that three people were killed and dozens injured after a white nationalists' rally and ensuing violent incidents in Charlottesville, which was described by civil rights groups as America's "largest hate gathering in decades."

August 15

The Chicago Tribune website reported that in the morning of August 12, Richard Hubbard III, an African American, was stopped by two white policemen when he drove through the Cleveland suburb of Ohio. Without obvious provocation, he was pressed down to the car and punched over by the policemen. The incident evoked strong criticism on the police's abuse of force.

August 22

The Huffington Post website reported that on August 16, when an Asian customer dined at a New York restaurant, she was referred by an employee as "Ching Chong," a racially insulting name, on a takeout receipt.

August 23

The UN News Center reported that for the violent incident in Charlottesville, Anastasia Crickley, Chairperson of UN Committee on the Elimination of Racial Discrimination, noted that: "We are alarmed by the racist demonstrations, with overtly racist slogans, chants and salutes by white nationalists, neo-Nazis, and the Ku Klux Klan, promoting white supremacy and inciting racial discrimination and hatred." She criticized the U.S. government for failing to clearly oppose the racially violent actions, calling for U.S. politicians and government officials to unequivocally and unconditionally reject and condemn racist hate speech and crimes in Charlottesville and throughout the country.

August 23

The Interception.com website reported two US-led coalition air strikes in Syria in March killed at least 84 civilians, including 30 children. The targets of the U.S. army were a school for the displaced in the Mansoura town on the outskirts of Tabqa and a market in Tabqa respectively.

SEPTEMBER

September 8

The Associated Press reported that six black police officers had filed complaints claiming their white supervisors were racist. The supervisors referred to black civilians as "scum" and called black civilian killings "thinning the herd."

September 10

The National Broadcasting Company (NBC) website reported a shooting rampage at a Plano home party on the night of Sept. 10, leaving nine dead and one injured.

September 13

The New York Times website reported that eleven people whose phones and laptops were searched at the U.S. airports and at the nation's northern border were suing the Department of Homeland Security. Several of the plaintiffs said they were intimidated. According to the most recent data available, there were nearly 15,000 searches from October 2016 to March 2017, compared with 8,383 in the same period a year before.

September 13

Over 40 million people live in poverty, with 18.5 million of them in extreme poverty, according to the latest data from the United States Census Bureau.

September 15

A report from *the New York Post* website told that a volunteer Ohio firefighter posted racist comments on social media which said if he had to choose between saving a dog and a black man from a burning building, he would save the dog first. "That's because one dog is more important than a million [expletive]," he wrote, using the n-word.

September 16

ABC news reported that on Sept. 15 night, 32 people were arrested when protesters took to the street in St. Louis after a white former police officer, Jason Stockley, who killed 24-year-old black man Lamar Smith with five shots in 2011, was acquitted earlier that day. "If you look like me, then you feel like there is no other way to express yourself in this kind of verdict. Time and time again, African-American men are killed by police, and nobody is held accountable," a protester was quoted as saying.

September 25

ABC News website reported that the Senate held a hearing on the Republican health care bill, known as the Graham-Cassidy bill. People from all over the United States and all walks of life lined up as early as 5 a.m., urging lawmakers to oppose the bill. Protesters in wheelchairs cried aloud with chants of "No cuts to Medicaid! Save our liberty!" Capitol Police officers struggled to remove people, with some sliding out of their wheelchairs and onto the floor. 181 protesters were arrested.

September 27

British newspaper *The Independent* reported on its website that the U.S. government had quietly announced that it was planning on continuing to collect social media information on immigrants in America. Cesar Cuauhtemoc Garcia Hernandez, an associate professor of law at the University of Denver's Sturm College of Law, told *The Independent* that monitoring social media accounts could have a chilling effect on free speech.

OCTOBER

October 1

The USA Today website reported that at least 59 people have been killed and over 500 injured in a mass shooting at a Las Vegas concert, considered the worst mass shooting in modern U.S. history.

October 4

The Chicago Tribune website reported that U.S. authorities have made more than 300 arrests at demonstrations over the Sept. 15 acquittal of former officer Jason Stockley in the fatal shooting of an African American. Protesters and civil liberties groups have accused the authorities of using heavy-handed tactics against demonstrators. And the American Civil Liberties Union of Missouri filed a lawsuit which accused police of unnecessarily using tear gas and pepper spray, arresting bystanders and journalists.

October 18

A research by the Pew Research Center showed that 57 percent of women said the country hasn't done enough to give women equal rights with men; 38 percent of women who said they have faced gender discrimination cited experiences related to hiring, pay or promotion; 26 percent said they have had their abilities questioned or were treated as if they weren't smart because of their gender; and ten percent cited sexual harassment.

October 25

The International Business Times website reported that a study from the Reflective Democracy Campaign found that 90 percent of all U.S. elected officials were white and 71 percent were men. With only the wealthy funding and communicating with the campaigns of elected officials, politicians were incentivized to make policy decisions that align with their donors' interests, not those of their broader constituency. Nick Nyhart, founding executive of voting rights advocacy group Every Voice, said "every cycle, there are fewer and fewer donors giving more and more of the money. The voices of everyday people get heard less and less each year. People who win under [the current system] don't promote policies that everyday people want to happen."

October 26

A study on the website of the Institute for Women's Policy Research showed that child care costs represent a large financial burden for parents who are in college. Washington State's child care assistance rules made it difficult for low-income students to access child care. And Washington was one of 11 states that require parents in postsecondary education to also work to be eligible for child care assistance.

October 31

The New York Post website reported that police arrested three men who smashed more than 40 headstones and spray-painted racial slurs on graves that had Asian names on them at a Queens cemetery in the summer of 2016.

NOVEMBER

November 3

The New York Daily News website reported that a racist attack on two Asian school board candidates in central New Jersey came in the form of a postcard with racist words. The postcard, which was mailed to residents in Edison, included photos of Jingwei (Jerry) Shi and Falguni Patel with "DEPORT" stamped over their faces.

November 5

The website of WHAM, a New York based station, reported that at least 26 were dead and 20 were injured in a mass shooting happened in a church in Sutherland Springs, Texas. Those shot range from 5 to 72 years old, and the incident was called the "worst mass shooting" in the state's history.

November 7

The Huffington Post website reported that New York Police Department detectives Eddie Martins and Richard Hall were accused of detaining and raping a woman in a police van after finding her in possession of marijuana and anti-anxiety pills.

November 8

The Huffington Post website reported that eighty percent of the political nominees the president has sent to the Senate have been men. Among the nominees for U.S. attorney, 41 were men and only one was woman.

November 8

The website of the American Civil Liberties Union reported that after a decade of collecting evidence, the prosecutor for the International Criminal Court, Fatou Bensouda, announced that she would take steps toward a full investigation into possible war crimes and crimes against humanity committed over the course of the armed conflict in Afghanistan since May 2003. In a 2016 report, the prosecutor's office revealed that it had reason to believe that members of the U.S. military "subjected at least 61 detained persons to torture, cruel treatment, outrages upon personal dignity" and members of the CIA "subjected at least 27 detained persons to torture, cruel treatment, outrages upon personal dignity and/or rape."

November 18

The Huffington Post website reported that a report released from the U.S. Sentencing Commission looked at federal prison sentences in the United States from Oct. 1, 2011 to Sept. 30, 2016, and found that black male offenders received sentences on average 19.1 percent longer than those of "similarly situated" white male offenders. Sentencing was just one part of the broader problem of racial discrimination in the criminal justice system: Black people were incarcerated in U.S. state prisons at more than five times the rate of white people.

November 20

The New Yorker website reported on the hugely imbalanced gender ratio in tech industry. Studies estimated that women make up only a quarter of employees and eleven percent of executives in the industry. In September, three women brought a class-action lawsuit on behalf of all female Google employees, accusing the company of "segregating" women into lower-paying jobs and of paying them less than their male counterparts for "substantially similar work."

November 20

The USA Today website reported that sexual harassment troubles mounted in statehouses around the country. Since 2016, at least 40 lawmakers in 20 states have been publicly accused by more than 100 people of some form of sexual misconduct or harassment. In Illinois and California, hundreds of people signed letters alleging widespread sexual harassment in state politics.

November 21

The Newsweek website reported that hundreds of thousands of Americans were being denied the right to vote because they are poor. In nine states, legislators have enacted laws that disenfranchise anyone with outstanding legal fees or court fines. In Alabama, more than 100,000 people who owe money – roughly 3 percent of the state's voting-age population – have been struck from voting rolls.

November 22

The BBC website reported that former USA Olympic gymnastics sports doctor Larry Nassar has been accused of sexually abusing more than 130 women, including several Olympic gold medalists.

November 24

The New York Times website reported that the elderly and disabled citizens of any age have faced several obstacles while voting. The results of a survey of 178 polling places showed that the great majority had impediments outside – like steep ramps or inadequate parking – or inside that could discourage or exclude disabled voters. Voting machines may not accommodate people who use wheelchairs or are visually impaired.

November 29

The Al Jazeera website reported that protests carried out by African Americans have been monitored by the U.S. government and have been seen as a potential threat, according to documents from the FBI and the US Department of Homeland Security.

DECEMBER

December 5

The BBC website reported that the U.S. Supreme Court had ruled the new U.S. administration's travel ban on six mainly Muslim countries could go into full effect. The decision was a boost for President Trump's policy against travelers from Chad, Iran, Libya, Somalia, Syria and Yemen. A federal judge in Hawaii said the policy "plainly discriminates based on nationality" in violation of "the founding principles of this nation."

December 6

According to *the Guardian* website, a study showed that 553,742 people in the United States were homeless on a single night in 2017. The homeless population of New York increased 4.1 percent. The poverty rate of California has reached 20.4 percent.

December 12

The VOA website reported a survey showing that nearly six in 10 Americans believe the level of government corruption rose in the year since U.S. President Donald Trump was elected and that the White House was now a more corrupt institution than Congress. The survey said 44 percent of Americans believed that the White House officials were corrupt, and 38 percent believe members of Congress were.

December 13

The Al Jazeera website reported that sexual harassment, assault and violence were widespread among women farm-workers in the United States, who number hundreds of thousands across the country. Many women had come forward with stories of sexual abuse at the hands of powerful men working in media, politics, sports and other areas. Many of the women didn't have legal status in the US, leaving them with little recourse to report abuse, seek legal recourse or get any other type of support. The nature of their work – seasonal, temporary and low-wage – also played a role. Sexual harassment and abuse at work was widespread in industries dominated by low wages. A 2016 survey of 500 women employed in Chicago-area hotels and casinos found that 58 percent of hotel workers and 77 percent of casino workers had been sexually harassed by a guest.

December 13

The website of ABC news reported that the new U.S. administration has not released any prisoners at the Guantanamo Bay and not added any to the list of cleared men who can go home, or to a third country, for resettlement.

December 14

The Independent website reported that Nils Melzer, the U.N. special rapporteur on torture, said torture was still being carried out at Guantanamo Bay and urged the United States to end its torture of detainees held at the Guantanamo Bay detention facility.

December 14

The website of CNN reported that U.S. service members have been accused of assaulting and raping Okinawans.

December 15

According to the Al Jazeera website, the Federal Communications Committee (FCC) voted to end the 2015 Open Internet Rules on December 14. The end broke the net neutrality rules, and allowed internet service providers to block and "throttle" certain data streams. It would also deepen the "digital divide" between the wealthy and low-income communities. Nyasia Valdez with Detroit's Equitable Internet Initiative in Southwest Detroit, said making the internet more expensive would further economically disadvantage poor people. "It would be so devastating and further exacerbate the inequality that's already there." A research showed that 94 percent of job recruiters used online means of finding candidates for work. Minority and lower-income populations in the US would experience joblessness at higher rates. With so many jobs recruiting online, the problem of unemployment is made worse.

December 15

The website of the United Nations Human Rights Office of the High Commissioner, released a report from Philip Alston, the UN Human Rights Council's special rapporteur on extreme poverty and human rights, who had spent two weeks touring America. According to Alston, "the American Dream was rapidly becoming the American Illusion." He said, "I met with many people barely surviving on Skid Row in Los Angeles. I witnessed a San Francisco police officer telling a group of homeless people to move on but having no answer when asked where they could move to. I heard how thousands of poor people get minor infraction notices which seem to be intentionally designed to quickly explode into unpayable debt, incarceration, and the replenishment of municipal coffers. I saw sewage-filled yards in states where governments don't consider sanitation facilities to be their responsibility. I saw people who had lost all of their teeth because adult dental care is not covered by the vast majority of programs available to the very poor. I heard about soaring death rates and family and community destruction wrought by opioids, and I met with people in Puerto Rico living next to a mountain of completely unprotected coal ash which rains down upon them, bringing illness, disability and death. "He pointed out that the United States had harnessed neither its wealth nor its power nor its technology to address the situation in which 40 million people continue to live in poverty. The youth poverty rate in the United States was the highest across the OECD with one quarter of youth living in poverty compared to less than 14 percent across the OECD. According to the World Income Inequality Database, the US had the highest Gini rate (measuring inequality) of all Western Countries. The United States was fast becoming a champion of inequality. Philip Alston warned that "the persistence of extreme poverty is a political choice made by those in power. With political will, it could readily be eliminated."

On the same day, *the Guardian* website reported that the "health gap" between the US and its peer countries continued to grow. The United States had much fewer doctors and hospital beds per person than the OECD average. Americans could expect to live shorter and sicker lives, compared to people living in any other rich democracy. Neglected tropical diseases, including Zika, were increasingly common in the United States. It had been estimated that 12 million Americans live with a neglected parasitic infection. The United States had the highest prevalence of obesity in the developed world. In terms of access to water and sanitation the US ranked 36th in the world.

December 17

The Al Jazeera website reported that the so-called "medical deserts" were becoming more common in the United States. Since 2010, more than 80 rural hospitals had been closed and hundreds more were at risk of shutting their doors.

December 18

The Huffington Post website reported that at least 15 women said Judge Alex Kozinski groped them, made inappropriate sexual comments, and/or showed them pornography.

December 18

According to the gunviolencearchive.org website, as of December 18, 2017, the total number of gun violence and crime incidents in the United States was 60,091, including 338 mass shooting incidents, causing total deaths of 15,182 and 30,619 injuries. 716 children aged 0 to 11 were killed or injured, and 3,178 teens aged 12 to 17 were killed or injured.

December 27

The Center for Responsive Politics website reported the latest figures on federal lobbying activity showing that the total spent on lobbying in 2017 reached 2.468 billion U.S. dollars, a new record high in the past five years.

December 31

The Washington Post website reported that 987 people have been shot and killed by police in 2017. According to monthly statistics, in 2017, the U.S. police shot 92 people dead in January; 100 in February; 76 in March; 67 in April; 74 in May; 84 in June; 94 in July; 82 in August; 70 in September; 85 in October; 84 in November; and 79 in December.

2017年美国的人权纪录

中华人民共和国国务院新闻办公室

2018年4月

导 言

当地时间4月20日，美国国务院发布《2017年国别人权报告》，继续扮演“人权卫士”，以道德裁判官自居，对他国国内事务和人权状况横加指责，妄言谬评，似乎在这个世界上只有美国的人权状况是最完美的。回顾2017年，稍有正义感的人们都会发现，美国自身的人权纪录依旧劣迹斑斑，并呈持续恶化的趋势。

——2017年10月1日晚，拉斯维加斯发生美国现代史上最为严重的枪击案，造成近60人死亡、800余人受伤。

——2017年8月，一些白人至上主义者聚集夏洛茨维尔市，高呼纳粹口号，举行被称为“几十年来最大的仇恨聚会”。

——美国《大西洋》月刊网站和《纽约时报》网站等报道，多项对美国学者的调查显示，大多数受访者认为近几十年来美国民主一直停滞不前，美国的民主正在被金钱淹没。

——普林斯顿大学政治学教授马丁·吉伦斯的研究表明，过去40年来美国的经济政策“强烈反映了最富有者的偏好，而与贫困人口和中等收入群体的偏好几乎没有任何关系”。

——美国全国免罪记录中心 2017 年 3 月 7 日发布的研究报告显示，非洲裔美国人被误判谋杀罪的可能性比白人高 7 倍，被误判毒品犯罪的可能性是白人的 12 倍。针对同样罪行，非洲裔男性罪犯的刑期比白人男性罪犯平均高 19.1%。

——美国经济政策研究所 2017 年 2 月 13 日发表的报告显示，白人家庭的平均财富比非洲裔家庭高 7 倍以上，白人家庭财富中位值比非洲裔家庭财富中位值高 12 倍以上，超过四分之一非洲裔家庭的净资产为零或负数。

——据英国《卫报》网站和联合国人权高专办网站 2017 年 12 月报道，美国有 5230 万人生活在“经济贫困社区”，约 1850 万人处于极度贫困状态。

——英国广播公司网站 2017 年 12 月 11 日报道，美国有 1330 万贫困儿童，占儿童总人口的 18%；美国城市研究所的数据显示，美国有近 900 万儿童在持续贫困的家庭中成长，占儿童总人口的 11.8%。

一、公民权利遭受严重侵犯

美国暴力犯罪攀升，枪支泛滥问题依然难解，枪击案件持续高发，警察暴力执法引发广泛抗议，政府肆意侵犯个人网络隐私权，人民的生命和自由受到严重威胁。

暴力犯罪居高不下。美国联邦调查局 2017 年 9 月发布的《2016 年美国犯罪报告》显示，2016 年美国共发生暴力犯罪约 120 万起，较 2015 年增加 4.1%；平均每十万居民中发生 386.3 起，较 2015 年增长 3.4%。与 2015 年相比，严重暴力伤害案增加 5.1%，谋杀案增加 8.6%，强奸案增加 4.9%。[注1]

枪支泛滥导致枪击事件持续高发。皮尤研究中心调查显示，至少三分之二的被调查者称他们的家庭有过枪支。[注2]美国联邦调查局《2016 年美国犯罪报告》显示，2016 年 73% 的凶杀案涉枪。[注3]美国枪支暴力档案室《2017 年枪支暴力伤亡统计》显示，截至 12 月 25 日，2017 年美国共发生枪击事件 60091 起，共造成 15182 人死亡、30619 人受伤，其中大规模枪击事件 338 起。[注4]2017 年 10 月 1 日晚，64 岁的白人男子史蒂芬·帕多克在拉斯维加斯从曼德勒海湾宾馆 32 层的房间向楼下露天演唱会 2 万多名观众开枪扫射。枪击持续了 10 至 15 分钟，造成近 60 人死亡、500 余人受伤。这是美国现代史上最为严重的枪击案。[注5]事后，警察在其酒店房间与家中共搜出 42 支枪、数千发子弹及爆炸物。11 月 5 日，得克萨斯州萨瑟兰泉镇发生恶性枪击案，至少造成 26 人死亡、20 人受伤，死伤者的年龄从 5 岁到 72 岁不等。

警察滥用执法权力。美国联邦调查局 2017 年发布的数据显示，2016 年美国执法部门共实施 10662252 次逮捕（不包括违反交通规则的逮捕），平均每十万居民中有 3298.5 人被逮捕。[注6]据《华盛顿邮报》网站统计，2017 年美国有 987 人被警察枪击致死。[注7]《华盛顿邮报》网站 2017

年7月26日报道，两名警察在执行逮捕令的过程中走错地址，枪杀了一名无辜者，而受害人并无任何犯罪记录。皮尤研究中心2017年1月11日披露，在过去两年中有近500名非洲裔美国人被警方枪杀。（注8）《赫芬顿邮报》网站2017年11月7日报道，纽约两名警员在搜查毒品的过程中，将一名藏有大麻的女子扣留在警车里并实施了轮奸。

警察暴力执法引发广泛抗议。2017年2月22日晚，数百人走上加利福尼亚州阿纳海姆市街头，抗议一天前一名不当值的洛杉矶警员在与几名青少年的争执中开枪。警方逮捕了23名抗议者。（注9）9月15日晚，因枪杀非洲裔男性的前白人警察杰森·斯托克利当日被无罪释放，圣路易斯市发生了严重的暴力抗议事件，32名示威者被捕。抗议者表示，“一次又一次，非洲裔美国人被警察杀害，但没有人对此承担责任。”（注10）

网络监控侵犯个人隐私。英国《每日邮报》网站2017年4月6日报道，推特公司2017年3月收到行政命令，要求其提供反对美国总统强硬移民政策的账户使用者的信息，政府并未给出任何理由。该公司认为，政府是在滥用法律。《纽约时报》网站2017年9月13日报道，2016年10月至2017年3月，美国边检强制搜查手机和电脑近15000次，比2015年同期的8383次大幅提升。英国《独立报》网站2017年9月27日报道，美国政府宣布将继续收集移民的社交媒体信息。丹佛大学法学副教授塞萨尔·赫尔南德斯认为，监控社交媒体账户会对言论自由产生可怕的影响。美国司法部对发生在总统就职日的抗议活动展开调查，要求“梦

的主人”公司交出负责协调抗议活动网站130万访问者的IP地址。（注11）

二、系统性种族歧视加剧社会撕裂

美国既有的种族歧视问题未见缓解，种族关系进一步恶化，社会对立加剧，种族冲突频发。

执法司法领域存在系统性的种族歧视。《赫芬顿邮报》网站2017年11月18日报道，美国量刑委员会2017年11月的报告发现，针对同样罪行，非洲裔男性罪犯的刑期比白人男性罪犯平均高19.1%。据美国全国免罪记录中心2017年3月7日发布的研究报告，对1989年至2016年10月被改判无罪案例的分析发现，非洲裔美国人比白人更容易被误判犯有谋杀罪、性侵犯、非法毒品活动等罪行。在1900名被宣判有罪但后来改判无罪的被告人中，非洲裔占47%，是其人口比例的3倍。（注12）斯坦福大学“警务公开项目”2017年6月19日发布研究报告，对美国20个州6000万次警察交通拦截数据的分析显示，警察在执法中对非洲裔、拉美裔司机适用与白人不同的标准，对他们进行搜查所需要的怀疑理由要远少于白人。非洲裔、拉美裔司机被警察拦截检查的可能性是白人的两倍。一旦被拦截，他们更容易被罚款、搜查乃至逮捕。例如，当因超速行驶而被要求靠边停车后，他们被开罚单的可能性比白人分别高20%和30%。（注13）“警察暴力地图”网站2018年1月1日发布的统计数据显示，美国警察2017年共杀死1129人，其中非洲裔占25%，远高于其13%的人口比例。

美国有线电视新闻网2017年9月1日报道，佐治亚州一名已有20年警龄的白人警官格雷格·阿伯特拦检一位白人女性司机，当被拦截的司机表示因担心警察开枪而不敢挪动双手时，阿伯特脱口而出："你不是黑人。记住，我们只杀黑人。"美联社2017年9月8日报道，费城警察局6名非洲裔警察对上级警官提出涉及种族主义的投诉，称这些白人警官将非洲裔公民称为"人渣"，将杀害非洲裔公民称为"减少牲畜存栏数"。

种族仇恨犯罪创近年新高。美国联邦调查局2017年11月13日公布的统计数据显示，2016年美国共发生6121起仇恨犯罪，达到了近年来未曾有过的高点。2016年11月美国总统选举后，种族主义口号和信息明显增长，特别是在学校中。南方贫困法律中心在选举日后的10天里发现了867起仇恨骚扰或恐吓事件。（注14）半岛电视台网站2017年6月10日报道，52岁的白人男子亚当·普林顿在堪萨斯州一个酒吧内高喊"滚出我的国家"，并对两名印度裔男子开枪射击，致一死一伤。《纽约邮报》网站2017年10月31日报道，3名男子涉嫌于2016年夏天在纽约皇后区公墓毁损40余块墓碑，并在带有亚裔姓名的墓碑上喷涂不堪入目的种族攻击性话语。

白人至上主义游行引发暴力冲突。2017年8月，一些白人种族主义者和右翼抗议者聚集在弗吉尼亚州的夏洛茨维尔市游行示威，高喊着"鲜血与土地"的纳粹战斗口号。（注15）20岁的白人至上主义者詹姆斯·菲尔茨驾驶汽车高速撞向抗议白人至上主义游行的人群，致使 1 人死亡、19 人受伤。[注 16]英国《每日电讯报》网站 2017 年 8 月 13 日报道，美国民权团体将这次白人至上主义游行描述为“几十年来最大的仇恨聚会”。针对这一事件，8 月 23 日联合国消除种族歧视委员会主席阿纳斯塔西娅·克里科里指出：“我们对白人民族主义者、新纳粹和三 K 党以公开的种族主义口号和仪式进行的种族主义游行感到极度震惊，这种行为助长了白人至上主义并煽动种族歧视和仇恨。”她对美国政府未能明确反对种族暴力行径提出了批评，并呼吁美国的政治家和政府官员对发生在夏洛茨维尔和全美国的种族仇恨演讲及犯罪予以无条件的、明确的谴责与抵制。[注 17]

种族关系恶化。盖洛普网站 2017 年 3 月 15 日发布的民意测验数据显示，42% 的美国民众表示对美国的种族关系感到极度担忧，比 2016 年高 7 个百分点。这是该数据连续第三年大幅增加，也是盖洛普调查 17 年来的最高纪录。皮尤研究中心 2017 年 8 月的调查结果显示，58% 的受访者认为种族主义是美国社会的一个大问题，比两年前增加了 8 个百分点，比 2011 年大约翻了一番。[注 18]英国广播公司网站 2017 年 9 月 26 日报道，2016 年美国职业橄榄球联盟非洲裔球星凯珀尼克在比赛现场播放美国国歌时拒绝起立，并以半跪的方式面对国旗。他表示：“我不会站起来去给一个压迫非洲裔和其他有色人种的国家的国旗致敬。”此后，许多美国职业橄榄球联盟球员纷纷加入他的行列。

种族歧视事件频繁发生。英国广播公司网站 2017 年 5 月 31 日报道，美国篮球职业联赛巨星勒布朗·詹姆斯在洛杉矶的住所被人喷涂了表示“黑鬼”的字母。他指出，种族主义永远是美国的一部分，在美国现实中，对非洲裔美国人的仇恨天天存在。《纽约邮报》网站 2017 年 9 月 15 日报道，俄亥俄州一名志愿消防队员在社交平台上发表种族主义言论，声称“在发生火灾的房子里，我宁愿选择先救狗而不是黑鬼”，“那是因为一只狗比一百万个（黑鬼）更重要”。《纽约每日新闻》网站 2017 年 11 月 3 日报道，新泽西州爱迪生市两名亚裔学校委员会候选人遭遇种族主义攻击，市民们收到印着这两位亚裔候选人照片的明信片，脸上被打上了种族主义口号。皮尤研究中心的调查显示，少数族裔群体更加频繁地遭遇带有种族歧视色彩的网络骚扰。四分之一的非洲裔和十分之一的拉美裔美国人表示因为种族或族裔的原因而在网络上受到骚扰。（注 19）

少数族裔群体在就业、薪酬等方面处于全方位的劣势。《洛杉矶时报》网站 2017 年 9 月 15 日报道，从美国劳工部 20 世纪 70 年代开始记录失业率以来，非洲裔的失业率一直接近于白人的两倍。旧金山联邦储备银行 2017 年 9 月 5 日发布的研究报告显示，1979 年非洲裔的时薪是白人的 80%，到 2016 年已经下降到 70%。（注 20）《今日美国报》网站 2017 年 12 月 16 日报道，在全国范围内，典型的非洲裔家庭的收入仅为普通白人家庭收入的 61%。在宾夕法尼亚州伊利市，白人失业率为 4%，非洲裔却高达 24.6%，非洲裔收入的中位值仅为白人的 43.2%。《今日美国报》网站 2017 年 10 月 3 日报道，所有少数族裔群体在高科技行业从业人员的比重都在下降。旧金山一家人力资源技术公司 2017 年 3 月 29 日发布的研究报告显示，虽然非洲裔和拉美裔劳动人口占美国劳动人口的比例都超过 12%，但非洲裔在白领劳动力中仅占 2%–3%，拉美裔仅占 5%。（注 21）

种族间财富差距日益扩大。美国联邦储备委员会 2017 年 9 月公布的数据显示，2013 年至 2016 年，非洲裔和拉美裔与白人之间的贫富差距分别增长了 16% 和 14%。2016 年美国白人家庭净资产中位值为 171000 美元，而非洲裔仅为 17600 美元，拉美裔为 20700 美元，分别为白人家庭的 10.29% 和 12.11%。（注 22）美国经济政策研究所 2017 年 2 月 13 日发表的报告显示，超过四分之一非洲裔家庭的净资产为零或负数。（注 23）美国人口普查局 2017 年 9 月公布的数据显示，2016 年非洲裔美国家庭收入中位值是 39490 美元，比 2000 年还低 1873 美元，是唯一收入低于 2000 年水平的种族群体。（注 24）

穆斯林遭受歧视与攻击。2017 年 1 月 27 日，美国政府发布一项行政命令，禁止伊朗、伊拉克、利比亚、索马里、苏丹、叙利亚和也门等 7 个国家的公民进入美国。由于禁令所涉国家均以穆斯林人口为主，因此该行政令也被普遍解读为“穆斯林禁令”。这一禁令在美国国内和世界各地都引发了广泛抗议。皮尤研究中心 2017 年初的一项调查显示，75% 的美国成年穆斯林表示美国社会存在大量对穆斯林的歧视，69% 的普通公众也持相同观点。50% 的穆斯林表示，近年来在美国做一名穆斯林变得更加困难。皮尤研究中心对美国联邦调查局仇恨犯罪统计数据的分析显示，

2015 年至 2016 年，在美国针对穆斯林的攻击事件数量显著增长，超过了 2001 年“9·11”事件后的峰值。(注 25)

三、美式民主存在严重弊端

美国金钱政治持续发酵，富人主导政治走向，弱势群体行使投票权面临更严苛的限制，政治人物丑闻频发。

金钱政治加剧不平等。英国《金融时报》网站 2017 年 7 月 15 日指出，“美国的政治体系已经被巨额资金所扭曲。”美国联邦选举委员会的数据显示，数十个政治行动委员会在 2017 年第一季度共筹集数千万美元的资金。个人捐助者向政治行动委员会和有关政治实体捐助了 2.364 亿美元，与 2013 年第一季度相比增加了约 30%。(注 26) 美国政治响应中心网站 12 月 27 日的数据显示，美国 2017 年的政治游说支出达到近五年来的最高值。(注 27)《纽约时报》网站 2017 年 9 月 20 日的评论称，“美国的民主正在被金钱淹没。”金钱政治使得美国过去 40 年的经济政策“强烈反映了最富有者的偏好，而与贫困人口和中等收入美国人的偏好几乎没有任何关系”。

民主政治走向衰退。一项对专家的调查显示，89% 的受访者认为过去 10 年来美国民主质量一直在下降。(注 28) 美国《大西洋》月刊网站 2017 年 6 月 21 日报道，一项关于美国民主状况的调查显示，大多数受访者认为，在给予公民平等的投票机会、阻止官员利用公职谋取私利以及民主决策等方面，美国政府是失败的。

低收入者的投票权受到更严苛的限制。美国《新闻周刊》网站2017年11月21日报道，成千上万的美国人因贫穷而被剥夺了投票权。已有9个州通过立法，剥夺任何未付律师费或法院罚款者的投票权。仅在亚拉巴马州，就有超过10万名欠费者被剔除出选民名单，约占该州选民人口的3%。文章评论道，“我们国家正处于有史以来富人比以往任何时候都更有政治权力的时代，不让欠律师费或法庭罚款的人投票，更是封住了低收入群体的口。”

老年人、残疾人行使投票权面临更多障碍。《纽约时报》网站2017年11月24日报道，美国投票站设置的投票机器很难被老年人或残疾人使用。一项针对178个投票站使用情况的调查显示，绝大多数投票站内外都存在通行障碍，如坡道过陡或车位不足，使残疾选民无法参与投票。

新闻媒体受到压制。2017年，多家媒体在参加政府新闻发布和官方活动报道时受到政府排斥，美国有线电视新闻网和《纽约时报》等一些媒体甚至被禁止参加白宫新闻发布会。2017年的一项调查报告显示，美国的新闻自由度跌至13年来最低点。（注29）皮尤研究中心2017年4月4日调查显示，73%的成年受访者认为美国现任政府与新闻媒体之间的紧张关系阻碍了他们获取国家的政治新闻和信息。（注30）

腐败丑闻爆发。2017年的一项调查显示，近六成美国人认为美国政府的腐败水平上升了，近七成受访者认为政府在反腐败方面是失败的。哥伦比亚广播公司新闻网站2017年3月14日报道，有9名军官因涉嫌卷入贿赂丑闻而受到起诉，其中包括已经退休的布鲁斯·拉夫莱斯上将。作为利益交换，他们接受了一名承包商提供的贿赂，包括妓女服务、奢华宴席和豪华旅游。该贿赂案目前已有超过20名前任或现任海军军官面临指控。

议员和政府官员不断曝出性骚扰丑闻。《今日美国报》网站2017年11月20日报道，自2016年以来，美国20个州中至少有40名议员被100多人公开指控有某种形式的性行为不端或性骚扰。半岛电视台网站2017年12月12日报道，民主党议员阿尔·弗兰肯等人受到有关性骚扰的指控。《华盛顿邮报》网站2017年12月21日报道，参议员办公室用财政资金来解决性骚扰或性歧视的指控，众议员办公室自2008年以来也至少参与处理了10起涉及性骚扰或性歧视的投诉。《华盛顿邮报》网站2017年12月1日发表评论文章称，多名政要被指控性骚扰却受到所属政党包庇，展示了美国政界的丑陋形象。

四、贫富分化现象持续恶化

美国贫富分化加剧，无家可归者人数增长，毒品和违禁药物泛滥，“医疗荒漠”地带蔓延，贫困人口生活悲惨。联合国人权理事会极端贫困和人权问题特别报告员菲利普·奥尔斯顿一针见血地指出：“美国梦正在迅速蜕变成美国幻想。”（注31）

贫困人口生活状况堪忧。英国《卫报》网站2017年12月8日报道，有5230万美国人生活在“经济贫困社区”，约占美国总人口的17%。美国人口普查局的统计数据显示，超过4000万美国人生活在贫困中，其中约1850万人处于极度贫困状态，其家庭收入低于贫困线的一半。（注32）斯坦福大学贫困与不平等问题研究中心2017年发布的报告显示，美国南部农村的整体贫困率为20%，其中非洲裔美国人的贫困率是33%，非洲裔妇女的贫困率高达37%。在美国西部农村，原住民的贫困率高达32%。（注33）联合国人权理事会极端贫困和人权问题特别报告员菲利普·奥尔斯顿在美国进行为期两周的实地考察后指出，美国是世界上最富有、最强大和最具科技创新能力的国家之一，但无论是财富、权力还是技术都没有被用来解决4000万人持续贫困的局面。他的结论是："极端贫困的持续存在是当权者作出的政治选择。"（注34）

不平等程度持续恶化。美国贫富分化的程度在不断加大。世界收入不平等数据库的数据显示，美国的基尼系数在西方国家中是最高的。在经济合作与发展组织37个成员国中，美国的贫困和不平等程度排第35位。（注35）德意志银行首席国际经济学家托斯坦·斯洛克以收入水平来计算美国家庭财富的报告显示，美国0.1%最富有家庭的财富相当于最底层90%家庭所拥有财富的总和。（注36）《波士顿评论》网站2017年9月1日报道，在过去40年，80%中低收入人口的收入仅增长了约25%，而20%高收入人口的收入却几乎翻了一番。联合国贫困和人权监测机构指责美国领导人试图把这个国家变成"极端不平等的世界冠军"。（注37）

无家可归者生活悲惨。英国《卫报》网站2017年12

月6日报道，美国有多达553742人至少有一夜无家可归，纽约无家可归者增长率高达4.1%。在洛杉矶县无家可归者的露营地，大约1800个露宿“穷街”街头的无家可归者晚上只能共用9个没有门的卫生间。（注38）马修·德斯蒙德在《被驱逐者》一书中指出，美国每年都有数百万人因交不起房租而被房东赶走，他们是真正被遗忘的贫困人口。（注39）

毒品及成瘾性药物管控不力。《医学报刊》新闻网站2017年6月13日报道，美国有770万人滥用违禁药物。美国有线电视新闻网2017年12月14日报道，40%的12年级学生、28%的10年级学生和12.9%的8年级学生在过去一年里使用过某种违禁药物。哥伦比亚广播公司网站2017年6月6日报道，2011年至2015年，仅在俄亥俄州就以处方的形式开出了约40亿颗阿片类药物，过量用药成为当今50岁以下美国人死亡的首要原因。据美国疾病控制和预防中心2017年12月发布的报告，2016年美国有超过63600人因用药过量而死亡。（注40）美国广播公司网站2017年12月12日报道，阿片类药物使用量剧增已迫使成千上万的儿童离开他们的家庭，2012年至2016年因毒品导致的寄养案件增加了32%。

医疗保障问题重重。联合国人权理事会极端贫困和人权问题特别报告员菲利普·奥尔斯顿在其报告中指出，美国与同等发展水平国家之间的“健康差距”继续拉大，其国民预期寿命更短，更容易得病身亡。（注41）英国《卫报》网站2017年12月15日报道，美国的医疗费用和医疗保险越来越贵，尤其是慢性疾病的治疗费用，从哮喘到癌症的药物价格不断创出历史新高。皮尤研究中心2017年12月14日发布的调查报告显示，自2015年以来，对政府保障医疗服务的正面评价下降了20%。（注42）

五、特定群体遭受歧视和人身侵犯

美国女性面临着明显的就业和职场歧视，儿童的贫困、健康和人身安全问题引人担忧，残疾人遭遇暴力侵害，广泛存在的性骚扰和性侵犯引发轰轰烈烈的抗议浪潮。

女性遭受性骚扰、性侵犯严重威胁。2017年10月，针对美国影视制作人哈维·温斯坦性侵多名女明星的丑闻，美国各界在社交媒体上发起名为“我也是（受害者）”的社会运动，鼓励受害者用这种方式抗议美国广泛存在的性骚扰和性侵犯，得到了百万余人响应。美国平等就业机会委员会发布的报告称，60%的女性在工作中遭受过性骚扰。（注43）英国广播公司网站2017年11月22日报道，前美国奥林匹克体操运动队医生拉里·纳萨尔被指控性侵接受其治疗的女运动员，受害者多达130多名，其中包括多名奥运金牌得主。《赫芬顿邮报》网站2017年12月18日报道，联邦上诉法院法官亚历克斯·科津斯基受到多名前女性职员对其不正当性行为的指控。美国国防部2017年5月发布的年度性侵犯报告显示，2016年军队中发生的性侵犯案件达14900件。（注44）《赫芬顿邮报》网站2017年12月15日报道，受害女性在提出指控后，其隐私得不到保证，生活在被认出的恐惧之中，这对受害人提出性侵犯指控产生了负面影响。

就业、职场性别歧视严重。美国劳工统计局发布的就业报告显示，2016年10月至2017年10月，美国零售业岗位共减少54300个，但男性和女性的遭遇却截然不同：女性失去了超过16万个职位，而男性却增加了10.6万个职位。（注45）皮尤研究中心的调查显示，57%的女性表示国家在保障男女平等权利方面做得不够，38%的女性列举了自己在雇佣、薪酬和晋升方面遭遇性别歧视的经历。（注46）

儿童人身权利面临严重威胁。美国联邦调查局2017年7月发布的统计数据显示，2016年度美国发生的针对10岁及以下儿童的人身伤害案件达68068起，针对11岁至15岁儿童的人身伤害案件达97588起，针对16岁至20岁青少年的人身伤害案件达159963起。其中涉及性侵犯罪案件共发生83611起。（注47）美国妇女政策研究所网站2017年11月28日披露，在夏威夷，近五分之一的高中女生遭受过校园欺凌，超过四分之一的女生报告称曾遭受过非自愿的性接触。

贫困儿童的健康状况令人担忧。英国广播公司网站2017年12月11日报道，美国贫困人口中约有1330万儿童，占儿童总人口的18%。美国有将近900万儿童在长期贫困的家庭中成长，占美国儿童总人口的11.8%。（注48）在哥伦比亚特区的一项公房居住者健康状况调查中，33%的成年受访者反映家中有一个孩子患有哮喘，21%反映有一个孩子超重，14%反映有一个孩子患有慢性病。（注49）

残疾人遭遇暴力侵害。美国司法统计局2017年7月发布的数据显示，2009 年至 2015 年，12 岁以上残疾人的暴力受害率至少是非残疾人的两倍，其中 2015 年超过 2.5 倍。残疾人遭受严重暴力犯罪的比率是非残疾人的三倍以上。（注 50）根据美国联邦调查局 2017 年发布的 2016 年仇恨犯罪统计数据，对 2016 年报告的 6063 起单一偏见案件的分析显示，1.2% 的人受到残疾偏见的驱使。（注 51）

六、继续粗暴侵犯他国人权

美国主导的军事行动造成他国大量平民伤亡，关塔那摩监狱依然非法监禁他国公民并实施酷刑。美国还制造网络战争工具，肆意侵入他国网络实施监控。

在叙利亚的军事行动造成大量平民伤亡。《纽约时报》网站 2017 年 6 月 19 日报道，美国政府“全面授权”在伊拉克和叙利亚的美军自主决定如何使用和使用多少武力，却放松对平民伤亡的监督、调查和问责，导致平民死亡人数不断攀升。《琼斯夫人》杂志网站 2017 年 8 月 6 日报道，美国领导的联军和美国海军陆战队几个月来在叙利亚各地轰炸了至少 12 所学校、15 座清真寺、15 座桥梁以及多处民用设施、医疗机构、文物古迹和难民营。联军战机还对等待过河以躲避战祸的家庭所乘坐的船只发动了一系列空袭，21 名平民被屠杀。（注 52）哥伦比亚《穆斯林时报》网站 2017 年 6 月 24 日报道，美国军方在上半年至少四次袭击了叙利亚政府军，其中包括 4 月对叙利亚机场的一次导弹袭击。美国政治分析家迈尔斯 · 赫尼希表示，美国对叙利亚发动

的军事行动违反了《联合国宪章》。(注53)

关塔那摩监狱长期非法关押外国人并实施酷刑。美国广播公司新闻网站2017年12月13日报道，美国新一届政府并没有释放关塔那摩监狱的囚犯，也没有公开任何获释人员或者无罪人员的名单。半岛电视台网站2017年9月22日报道，在美洲人权委员会的听证会上，前关塔那摩被羁押者杰蒙·阿姆基恩表示，他在关塔那摩监狱被关押了11年，被长期单独监禁并经受多种形式的酷刑，却从未收到过任何关于其拘禁合法性的司法裁决。《今日美国报》网站2017年12月13日报道，联合国和国际人权组织批评美国在关塔那摩创造了一个“合法黑洞”，允许自己在那里无限期拘禁嫌疑人却不提起诉讼，甚至将很多未经审判的被羁押者长期羁押达十年以上。联合国人权理事会酷刑问题特别报告员尼尔斯·梅尔泽2017年12月13日敦促美国停止对关塔那摩监狱内被拘禁者施行酷刑。(注54)

制造网络战争武器。维基解密网站称，美国国家安全局已经侵入巴基斯坦的移动网络，并一直在监视该国数百个IP地址。(注55)“零对冲”网站2017年5月14日披露，美国国家安全局创建了一个被称为“绝命武器”的网络战争工具，它可以使任何人从后门溜入任何计算机系统。这一工具被黑客组织利用制作勒索病毒，发动了一场全球性的恶意网络攻击，劫持了全球20万个计算机系统。(注56)

注 释

（注 1）美国联邦调查局网站（https://www.fbi.gov，https://ucr.fbi.gov），2017 年 9 月。

（注 2）皮尤社会趋势网站（http://www.pewsocialtrends.org），2017 年 6 月 22 日。

（注 3）美国联邦调查局网站（https://ucr.fbi.gov），2017 年 9 月。

（注 4）美国枪支暴力档案室网站（http://www.gunviolencearchive.org），2017 年 12 月 25 日。

（注 5）英国广播公司网站(http://www.bbc.com),2017 年 10 月 2 日。

（注 6）美国联邦调查局网站（https://ucr.fbi.gov），2017 年 9 月。

（注 7）《华盛顿邮报》网站（https://www.washingtonpost.com）。

（注 8）皮尤社会趋势网站（http://www.pewsocialtrends.org），2017 年 1 月 11 日。

（注 9）《华盛顿邮报》网站（https://www.washingtonpost.com），2017 年 2 月 23 日。

（注 10）美国广播公司网站（http://abcnews.go.com），2017 年 9 月 16 日。

（注 11）美国有线电视新闻网（http://edition.cnn.com），2017 年 8 月 17 日。

（注 12）半岛电视台网站（http://www.aljazeera.com），2017 年 3 月 8 日。

（注 13）《洛杉矶时报》网站（http://www.latimes.com），2017 年 6 月 19 日。

（注 14）美国有线电视新闻网（http://edition.cnn.com），2017 年 11 月 13 日。

（注 15）美国有线电视新闻网（http://edition.cnn.com），2017 年 8 月 12 日。

（注 16）哥伦比亚广播公司新闻网（https://www.cbsnews.com），2017 年 8 月 12 日。

（注 17）联合国网站（http://www.un.org），2017 年 8 月 23 日。

（注 18）皮尤研究中心网站（http://www.pewresearch.org），2017 年 8 月 29 日。

（注 19）皮尤研究中心网站（http://www.pewresearch.org），2017 年 7 月 25 日。

（注 20）《华盛顿邮报》网站（https://www.washingtonpost.com），2017 年 9 月 5 日。

（注 21）《国际财经时讯》网站（http://www.ibtimes.com），2017 年 3 月 31 日。

（注 22）《华盛顿邮报》网站（https://www.washingtonpost.com），2017 年 9 月 28 日。

（注 23）经济政策研究所网站（http://www.epi.org），2017 年 2 月 13 日。

（注 24）《洛杉矶时报》网站（http://www.latimes.com），2017 年 9 月 15 日。

（注 25）皮尤研究中心网站（http://www.pewresearch.org），2017 年 11 月 15 日。

（注 26）《商业杂志》网站（https://www.bizjournals.com），2017 年 5 月 8 日。

（注 27）"秘密公开"网站（https://www.opensecrets.org），2017 年 12 月 27 日。

（注 28）authwarningsurvey 网站（https://www.authwarningsurvey.com），2017 年 6 月 28 日。

（注 29）美国有线电视新闻网（http://www.cnn.com），2017 年 4 月 28 日。

（注 30）“新闻学”网站（http://www.journalism.org），2017 年 4 月 4 日。

（注 31）英国《卫报》网站（https://www.theguardian.com），2017 年 12 月 15 日。

（注 32）联合国人权高专办网站（http://www.ohchr.org），2017 年 12 月 15 日。

（注 33）斯坦福大学贫困与不平等研究中心网站（https://inequality.stanford.edu）。

（注 34）英国《卫报》网站（https://www.theguardian.com），2017 年 12 月 15 日。

（注 35）英国《卫报》网站（https://www.theguardian.com），2017 年 12 月 15 日。

（注 36）“商业内幕”网站（http://www.businessinsider.com），2017 年 1 月 25 日。

（注 37）英国《卫报》网站（https://www.theguardian.com），2017 年 12 月 15 日。

（注 38）英国《卫报》网站（https://www.theguardian.com），2017 年 6 月 30 日。

（注 39）英国《卫报》网站（https://www.theguardian.com），2017 年 2 月 24 日。

（注 40）美国疾病控制和预防中心网站（https://www.cdc.gov）。

（注 41）英国《卫报》网站（https://www.theguardian.com），2017 年 12 月 15 日。

（注 42）people−press 网站（http://www.people−press.org），2017 年 12 月 14 日。

（注 43）《今日美国报》网站（https://www.usatoday.com），2017 年 12 月 8 日。

（注 44）美国广播电视公司第 7 频道网站（http://abc7ny.com），2017 年 12 月 13 日。

（注 45）美国妇女政策研究所网站（https://iwpr.org），2017 年 12 月 18 日。

（注 46）皮尤社会趋势网站（http://www.pewsocialtrends.org），2017 年 10 月 18 日。

（注 47）美国联邦调查局网站（https://ucr.fbi.gov）。

（注 48）mobilitypartnership 网站（http://www.mobilitypartnership.org），2017 年 5 月 18 日。

（注 49）美国城市研究所网站（http://www.mobilitypartnership.org），2017 年 3 月 6 日。

（注 50）美国司法统计局网站（https://www.bjs.gov）。

（注 51）美国联邦调查局网站（https://ucr.fbi.gov）。

（注 52）《琼斯夫人》杂志网站（http://www.motherjones.com），2017 年 8 月 6 日。

（注 53）哥伦比亚《穆斯林时报》网站（http://muslimtimes.co），2017 年 6 月 24 日。

（注 54）《今日美国报》网站（https://www.usatoday.com），2017 年 12 月 13 日。

（注 55）《经济时报》网站（https://economictimes.indiatimes.com），2017 年 4 月 11 日。

（注 56）“零对冲”网站（http://www.zerohedge.com），2017 年 5 月 14 日。

附录：2017 年美国侵犯人权事记

一月

6 日　美联社网站报道，在罗德岱堡机场，一名退役军人从已通过安检的行李中取出枪支射击，导致 5 人死亡、8 人受伤。

11 日　皮尤研究中心披露，自 2015 年以来，近 500 名非洲裔美国人被警方枪杀，引发了民众对美国警察的普遍抗议。

27 日　美国政府发布行政命令，要求至少暂停四个月安置全世界难民，对于叙利亚难民则要无限期延长，至少 90 天内阻止伊朗、伊拉克、利比亚、索马里、苏丹、叙利亚和也门的签证持有人入境。

28 日　美国各地爆发示威活动，抗议白宫关于中止难民和一些伊斯兰国家居民入境的行政命令。

31 日　《今日美国报》网站报道，27 名来自美国各地的原告提出诉讼，称美国政府中止难民和一些伊斯兰国家居民入境的行政命令是“穆斯林禁令”，“它以宗教信仰为基础，将外国国民分为受欢迎和不受欢迎的群体，其中甚至包括在美国境内合法居住的人，这是对特定信仰的人的一种不公正对待”。

二月

13 日　美国经济政策研究所发布报告显示，白人家庭的平均财富比非洲裔家庭平均财富高 7 倍以上，白人家庭财富中位值比非洲裔家庭财富中位值高 12 倍以上。超过四分之一非洲裔家庭的净资产为零或负数，而白人家庭的这一比例则不到十分之一。

21 日　福布斯新闻网报道，学生贷款债务成为排名第二的消费债务类别，高于信用卡和汽车贷款。美国有超过 4400 万的学生贷款人，贷款总额高达 1.3 万亿美元。2016 级学生人均贷款 37172 美元。

22 日　美国有线电视新闻网报道，自 1 月 20 日以来，共有 214 人因参加在华盛顿市区的总统就职日抗议活动而被以重罪起诉。

23 日　《华盛顿邮报》网站报道，2 月 22 日晚，数百人走上加利福尼亚州阿纳海姆市街头，抗议一天前一名不当值的洛杉矶警员在与几名青少年的争执中开枪，23 人被逮捕。

24 日　英国《卫报》网站报道，美国新一届政府就职后，立即取消了降低房屋保险费 0.25% 的政策，使得大量中等收入家庭的生活变得更糟糕。美国每年有数百万人被赶出租住的房屋，这些人是真正被遗忘的穷人。

三月

6日　美国城市研究所的研究报告显示，住在公共房屋的家庭中，33%的家庭有一个家庭成员年龄在62岁以上，39%的家庭有儿童，21%的居住者身患残疾。在一项哥伦比亚特区公房居住者健康状况的调查中，33%的成年受访者反映有一个孩子患有哮喘，21%反映有一个孩子超重，14%反映有一个孩子患有慢性病。

7日　美国全国免罪记录中心发布研究报告，对1989年至2016年10月被改判无罪案例的分析发现，非洲裔美国人比白人更容易被误判犯有谋杀罪、性侵犯、非法毒品活动等罪行。在1900名被宣判有罪但后来改判无罪的被告人中，非洲裔占47%，是其人口比例的3倍。

14日　美国哥伦比亚广播公司新闻网站报道，有9名军官因涉嫌卷入贿赂丑闻而受到起诉，其中包括已经退休的布鲁斯·拉夫莱斯上将。作为利益交换，他们接受了一名承包商提供的贿赂，包括妓女服务、奢华宴席和豪华旅游。该贿赂案目前已有超过20名前任或现任海军军官面临指控。

15日　盖洛普民意调查显示，42%的受访者表示对美国的种族关系感到极度担忧，比2016年高出7个百分点。这是盖洛普调查17年来的最高纪录，也是对这一问题担忧的受访者比例连续第三年大幅增加。

15日　美国政策研究所网站报道，2016年华尔街银行向17.7万名纽约员工发放了239亿美元奖金，这是全美107.5万名全职最低工资工人年收入的1.6倍。自1985以来，华尔街平均奖金增加了 890%，而全美最低工资仅上升了 116%。

28 日　《华盛顿邮报》网站报道，美国国会提出取消在线隐私保护措施的立法建议，对互联网准入规则进行重大修改。一旦获得批准，互联网服务提供商就可以对客户的行为进行在线监控，并且在未经客户许可的情况下，使用他们的个人和财务信息销售精准投放的广告。数字民主中心执行主任杰弗里·切斯特认为，这意味着美国人永远不能安全上网，因为他们最隐私的细节被监控并被偷偷卖给了出价最高的人，这是“巨大的倒退”。

四月

4 日　《今日美国报》网站报道，妇女政策研究所的统计数据显示，美国全职女性周薪仅为全职男性的 82%。非洲裔和拉美裔女性的收入仅为白人男性的 68% 和 62%。

6 日　英国《每日邮报》网站报道，推特公司 2017 年 3 月收到行政命令，要求其提供反对美国总统强硬移民政策的账户使用者的信息，政府并未给出任何理由。该公司认为，政府是在滥用法律。

11 日　《经济时报》网站报道，维基解密网站披露，美国国家安全局已经侵入巴基斯坦的移动网络，并一直在监视该国数百个 IP 地址。

11 日　《华盛顿邮报》网站报道，美国联合航空公司工作人员因机票超售强行将一位亚裔乘客拖下飞机，致其血流满面。有人听到该乘客抱怨说因为自己是亚裔才遭到如此对待。

30日　英国《独立报》网站报道，美国国防部称，2014年以来，美国领导的对伊拉克和叙利亚的空袭造成至少352名平民遇难。而据空中战争跟踪组织统计，空袭造成的平民死亡人数超过3000名。

五月

8日　美国联邦选举委员会的数据显示，数十个政治行动委员会在2017年前三个月中筹集了数千万美元的资金。个人捐助者向政治行动委员会和有关政治实体捐助了2.364亿美元，与2012年总统选举后同一时期相比增长约30%。

11日　英国《太阳报》网站报道，美国非洲裔女性拉内·鲍德温购买了两张美国航空公司头等舱机票，5月2日与白人朋友一起从肯塔基州飞往北卡罗来纳州，但在登机后却被告知没有足够的头等舱座位，她的白人朋友被安排在了头等舱，而她自己却被要求到机舱后部就座。

11日　《国会山报》网站报道，美国人口普查局5月10日公布的数据显示，2016年美国总统选举中，合格选民投票的比例为61.4%，降至16年来的最低水平。只有49%的亚裔选民和47.6%的拉美裔选民参与了投票；非洲裔选民的投票率为59.4%，比2012年下降了近7个百分点。

14日　“零对冲”网站披露，美国国家安全局创建了一个被称为“绝命武器”的网络战争工具，它可以使任何人从后门溜入任何计算机系统。这一工具被黑客组织利用制作勒索病毒，发动了一场全球性的恶意网络攻击，劫持了全球 20 万个计算机系统。

15 日　皮尤研究中心网站报道，根据美国人口普查局发布的数据，2016 年 11 月美国成年人数为 24550 万，其中约有 15760 万人为注册选民。按照国际标准的投票年龄人口计算，2016 年美国总统选举的投票率仅为 55.7%，落后于经济合作与发展组织的大部分国家。

17 日　美国平等就业机会委员会网站披露，卡罗莱纳克里克公司在得知员工克里尔·里德患有妊娠并发症后，将她降职。此举违反了联邦反歧视法。里德向公司执行董事申诉将其降职违法，公司反而解雇了她，并对她提起两项诉讼。

31 日　英国广播公司网站报道，美国篮球巨星勒布朗·詹姆斯在洛杉矶的住宅被人喷涂表示“黑鬼”的字母。他坦言，“在美国，无论你多么有钱，多么出名，……但只要你是非洲裔，就会处境艰难”；“种族主义永远是美国的一部分，在美国现实中，对非洲裔的仇恨天天存在”。

六月

1 日　《华盛顿邮报》网站报道，美国宣布将退出应对全球气候变化的《巴黎协定》。评论认为这是毫无道理的，气候变化对美国人健康的威胁是真实存在的，而政府却仅仅从美国的经济利益角度来看待这一国际协定。

9 日　美国有线电视新闻网报道，芝加哥 23 岁白人男子威廉·布彻无故对非洲裔吐口水，称非洲裔为“黑奴”，辱骂非洲裔孩子是“该死的寄生虫”。

10日　半岛电视台网站报道，52岁的白人男子亚当·普林顿在堪萨斯州一个酒吧内高喊“滚出我的国家”，并对两名印度裔男子开枪射击，致一死一伤。

21日　美国《大西洋》月刊网站报道，多项对美国学者的调查显示，大多数受访者认为，近几十年来美国民主一直停滞不前，在给予公民平等的投票机会、阻止官员利用公职谋取私利等方面，美国政府是失败的。

22日　《圣迭戈联合论坛报》网站报道，残疾人权益组织发起抗议活动，反对削减医疗补助资金。组织者布鲁斯·达林发布声明说，美国医疗保险法案限制并大幅削减医疗补助计划，这将使那些靠此度日的老年人和残疾人无法享受所需的基本医疗服务。

30日　英国《卫报》网站报道，最新统计显示，洛杉矶县的无家可归者人数增加了23%，达到57794人。对于露宿“穷街”街头的1800名无家可归者而言，晚上仅有9个没有门的卫生间可供使用。

七月

5日　英国《金融时报》网站文章指出，“美国的政治体系已经被巨额资金所扭曲”，它已被共和党精英的寡头政治控制，主要对超富裕的捐款者负责。富人捐款者通过操纵选举等行为成功地创造了这样的局面：即使他们不能控制所有的政府部门，也能够占据重要位置，有效地阻断任何试图改变现状的议程。

11日　皮尤研究中心公布的数据显示，18岁至29岁的人中约有 67% 经历过某种形式的网上骚扰。年轻女性更有可能成为网上性骚扰的对象。18 岁至 29 岁的女性中有 21% 表示她们受到过网上性骚扰，有 53% 表示收到过不期而至的色情图片。

22 日　美国“截击”网站报道，美国正在重新升级在阿富汗的战争，扩大在伊拉克和叙利亚的军事行动，在索马里和也门开展秘而不宣的军事打击。

22 日　英国《独立报》网站报道，美国在 7 月 21 日的空袭中击中正在与塔利班作战的阿富汗警察，造成 16 名阿富汗警察死亡，另有 2 人受伤。

25 日　皮尤研究中心的调查显示，美国少数族裔群体更加频繁地遭遇带有种族歧视色彩的网络骚扰。四分之一的非洲裔表示因为种族或族裔的原因在网络上受到过骚扰。74% 的非洲裔和 72% 的拉美裔认为网络骚扰是一个“大问题”。68% 的非洲裔表示在网络上感到安全和受欢迎比自由言论更重要。

26 日　《华盛顿邮报》网站报道，两名警察在执行逮捕令的过程中走错地址，枪杀了一名无辜者，而受害人并无任何犯罪记录。

八月

5 日　英国《卫报》网站报道，国际移民组织统计显示，2017 年前 7 个月从墨西哥跨越美国边境的移民死亡人数为 232 人，同比增加了 17%。

6 日　《琼斯夫人》杂志网站报道，美国领导的联军在叙利亚拉卡郊区非法使用白磷弹药，涉嫌构成战争罪。

12 日　美国有线电视新闻网报道，一些白人种族主义者和右翼抗议者聚集在夏洛茨维尔市游行示威，高喊“鲜血与土地”的纳粹战斗口号。

12 日　哥伦比亚广播公司网站报道，20 岁的白人至上主义者詹姆斯·菲尔茨驾驶汽车高速撞向抗议白人至上主义游行的人群，致使 1 人死亡、19 人受伤。

13 日　英国《每日电讯报》网站报道，夏洛茨维尔市白人至上主义游行及后续暴力事件共造成 3 人死亡、数十人受伤。美国民权团体将其描述为“几十年来最大的仇恨聚会”。

15 日　《芝加哥论坛报》网站报道，8 月 12 日早晨，非洲裔司机理查德·哈伯德和同伴开车穿过俄亥俄州的克利夫兰郊区时，被两名白人警察拦截检查，在他们没有明显挑衅的情况下，警察将其按倒在车上，反复用拳头殴打。该事件引发了对警察滥用武力的强烈质疑。

22 日　《赫芬顿邮报》网站报道，8 月 16 日，一名亚裔女顾客在纽约一家餐厅用餐时，发现餐厅员工将极具种族侮辱性的“中国佬”称呼作为顾客姓名打在收据上。

23 日　联合国新闻中心网站报道，针对在夏洛茨维尔发生的暴力事件，联合国消除种族歧视委员会主席阿纳斯塔西娅·克里科里指出：“我们对白人民族主义者、新纳粹和三 K 党以公开的种族主义口号和仪式进行的种族主义游行感到极度震惊，这种行为促进了白人至上主义并煽动种族歧视和仇恨。”她对美国政府未能明确反对种族暴力行径提出了批评，并呼吁美国的政治家和政府官员对发生在夏洛茨维尔和全美国的种族仇恨演讲和犯罪予以无条件的、明确的谴责与抵制。

23 日　“截击”网站报道，3 月美国领导的在叙利亚的两次联合空袭造成至少 84 名平民死亡，其中包括 30 名儿童。美军袭击目标分别是塔布卡郊外曼苏拉镇的流离失所者学校和塔布卡的市场。

九月

8 日　美联社报道，6 名非洲裔警察投诉白人上级警官为种族主义者，这些白人警官称非洲裔公民为“人渣”，并将杀害非洲裔民众称为“降低牲畜存栏数”。

10 日　美国全国广播公司网站报道，9 月 10 日晚上在普莱诺的一个家庭聚会中发生枪击事件，造成 9 人死亡、1 人受伤。

13 日　《纽约时报》网站报道，11 人因手机和笔记本电脑在美国机场和北部边境被搜查而对国土安全部提起诉讼，其中部分原告称他们被威胁。据统计，2016 年 10 月至 2017 年 3 月期间，美国边检强制打开手机和电脑进行内容检查近 15000 次，而去年同期只有 8383 次。

13 日　美国人口普查局最新统计数据显示，超过 4000 万人生活在贫困之中，约有 1850 万人生活在极度贫困之中。

15 日　《纽约邮报》网站报道，俄亥俄州一名志愿消防队员在社交平台上发表种族主义言论，声称“在发生火灾的房子里，我宁愿选择先救狗而不是黑鬼”，“那是因为一只狗比一百万个（黑鬼）更重要”。

16日　美国广播公司网站报道，9月15日晚，因枪杀非洲裔男性的前白人警察杰森·斯托克利当日被无罪释放，圣路易斯市发生了严重的暴力抗议事件，32名示威者被捕。斯托克利于2011年连开5枪射杀了24岁的安东尼·拉马尔·史密斯。抗议者表示，“如果你和我一样是非洲裔美国人，那么你也会觉得没有其他的方式来表达自己对这种判决的不满。一次又一次，非洲裔美国人被警察杀害，但没有人对此承担责任”。

25日　美国广播公司网站报道，参议院当日对共和党医疗保健法案举行听证会。从早上5点开始，来自全国各地、各行各业的人们排成长队准备入场，呼吁立法者否决该法案。坐在轮椅上的残疾抗议者高喊“不得削减医疗补助计划！拯救我们的自由！”他们被强行移走，有些残疾人从轮椅中滑落，倒在地上。有181名抗议者被捕。

27日　英国《独立报》网站报道，美国政府宣布将继续收集移民的社交媒体信息。丹佛大学斯特姆法学院法学副教授塞萨尔·赫尔南德斯认为，监控社交媒体账户会对言论自由产生可怕的影响。

十月

1日　《今日美国报》网站报道，美国拉斯维加斯的一场室外音乐会发生枪击案，造成59人死亡、500多人受伤，这是美国现代史上最为严重的一起枪击案件。

4日　《芝加哥论坛报》网站报道，枪杀非洲裔男性的前白人警察杰森·斯托克利被无罪释放引发抗议活动，当局逮捕了300多名示威者。抗议者和民权团体指责当局对示威者采取高压手段。密苏里州的美国民权联盟提起诉讼，指控警方毫无必要地使用催泪瓦斯和胡椒喷雾，逮捕旁观者和记者。

18日　皮尤研究中心发布的调查数据显示，57%的女性表示美国在男女平权方面做得不够。38%的女性表示自己曾遭遇过性别歧视，并列举了有关雇佣、薪资或晋升的经历；26%的女性表示曾因性别而被质疑能力或智力不足；10%的女性表示遭受过性骚扰。

25日　《国际财经时讯》网站撰文指出，“反思民主运动”的最新调查发现，美国90%的当选官员是白人，71%是男性。由于竞选资金主要来自于富人阶层捐赠，政治家制定的政策会更加符合其捐赠者而不是更广大选民的利益。选举权倡导组织“人人发声”的创始人尼克·尼哈特指出，“每一次竞选，捐赠者越来越少，而捐赠的资金越来越多。越来越难听到普通百姓的声音。那些在当前体制下赢得竞选的人不会推行普通百姓所期望的政策。”

26日　美国妇女政策研究所网站报道，托儿费用对于还在上大学的父母而言是一笔巨大的经济负担。华盛顿州制定的儿童保育援助规则过于严苛，使得正在接受高等教育的低收入家长难以获得托儿服务。该州系要求家长在接受高等教育的同时必须工作才能获得儿童保育援助的11个州之一。

31日　《纽约邮报》网站报道，3名男子涉嫌于2016年夏天在纽约皇后区公墓毁损40余块墓碑，并在带有亚裔姓名的墓碑上喷涂不堪入目的种族攻击性话语。

十一月

3日　《纽约每日新闻》网站报道，新泽西州爱迪生市两名亚裔学校委员会候选人遭遇种族主义攻击。爱迪生市居民收到印着两位亚裔候选人照片的明信片，他们的脸上被打上了“驱逐出境”的印章，并写上了种族主义口号。

5日　纽约州罗切斯特广电传媒网站报道，美国得克萨斯州萨瑟兰泉镇发生枪击案，至少造成26人死亡、20人受伤，死伤者的年龄从5岁到72岁不等。该州州长称这是该州历史上“最严重的枪击案”。

7日　《赫芬顿邮报》网站报道，纽约警察局的两名警探埃迪·马丁斯和理查德·霍尔被控在发现一名女子藏有大麻和抗焦虑药片后，将其扣留在警车里，并实施了轮奸。

8日　《赫芬顿邮报》网站报道，美国现任总统提交参议院审议的政府高官人选中男性比例高达80%，提名的检察官人选中41名是男性，只有1名女性。

8日　美国民权联盟网站报道，国际刑事法院检察官法图·本苏达在收集了十年的证据后，宣布将采取措施全面调查2003年5月以来美国在阿富汗武装冲突期间涉嫌犯下的战争罪和危害人类罪。该检察官在2016年的一份报告中披露，有理由相信美国军方对“至少61名被拘禁者实施了酷刑、虐待、侵犯人格尊严”，中央情报局成员对“至少27名被拘禁人员实施了酷刑、虐待、侵犯人格尊严或强奸”。

18日　《赫芬顿邮报》网站报道，美国量刑委员会发布了一份报告，对 2011 年 10 月 1 日到 2016 年 9 月 30 日联邦监狱徒刑判决情况进行审查，发现针对同样罪行，非洲裔男性罪犯刑期比白人男性罪犯刑期平均高 19.1%。判决不公只是刑事司法系统中种族歧视问题的冰山一角，在美国，被监禁的非洲裔是白人的五倍还多。

20 日　《纽约客》网站报道，科技行业的性别比例极不平衡。女性只占员工总数的四分之一，只占行业高管的 11%。9 月，三名女性代表全体谷歌女性员工提起集体诉讼，指控该公司将女性隔离于低薪工作区以及对同类工作支付的工资少于男性。

20 日　《今日美国报》网站撰文指出，美国各州议会深陷性骚扰丑闻。自 2016 年以来，20 个州中至少有 40 名议员被 100 多人公开指控有某种形式的性行为不端或性骚扰。伊利诺伊州和加利福尼亚州有数百人签署了声明，指控当地政界普遍存在性骚扰问题。

21 日　美国《新闻周刊》网站报道，成千上万的美国人因贫穷而被剥夺了投票权。已有 9 个州通过立法，剥夺任何未付律师费或法院罚款者的投票权。仅在亚拉巴马州，就有超过 10 万名欠费者被剔除出选民名单，约占该州选民人口的 3%。

22 日　英国广播公司网站报道，前美国奥林匹克体操运动队医生拉里·纳萨尔被指控性侵接受其治疗的女运动员，受害者达 130 多名，其中包括多名奥运金牌得主。

24 日　《纽约时报》网站报道，美国老年和残疾选民行使投票权过程中遭遇诸多障碍。一项针对 178 个投票站使用情况的调查显示，绝大多数投票站内外都存在通行障碍，如坡道过陡或车位不足。另外，投票机很难被坐在轮椅上的人或视障人士使用。

29 日　半岛电视台网站报道，美国联邦调查局和美国国土安全部公布的文件显示，美国政府正在监视非洲裔美国人的抗议活动，并将其视为潜在的威胁。

十二月

5 日　英国广播公司网站报道，美国最高法院裁定美国政府对来自乍得、伊朗、利比亚、索马里、叙利亚和也门等国家人员的旅行禁令全面生效。夏威夷的一位联邦法官表示，这项政策“明显基于国籍歧视”，违反了“这个国家的建国原则”。

6 日　英国《卫报》网站报道，2017 年美国有 553742 人至少有一夜无家可归。纽约无家可归者增长了 4.1%，加利福尼亚州的贫困率高达 20.4%。

12 日　美国之音网站报道，最新调查显示，接近六成的美国人认为，2017 年政府腐败水平上升，白宫现在是一个比国会更腐败的机构。在受访者中，44% 认为白宫官员是腐败分子，38% 认为国会议员腐败。

13 日　半岛电视台网站报道，在全美国数十万的女性农场工人中，性骚扰、殴打和暴力非常普遍。更多的女性说出在媒体、政治、体育和其他领域的有权势的男性手下遭遇性虐待的事情。许多女性在美国没有合法身份，没有办法举报虐待行为，也没有办法寻求法律或者其他任何形式的帮助。她们所从事的季节性、临时性和低工资性质的工作也妨碍了她们的举报。在低薪行业，工作中的性骚扰和虐待现象十分普遍。2016 年对芝加哥地区酒店和赌场的 500 名女性进行的一项调查发现，58% 的酒店工作人员和 77% 的赌场工作人员遭到客人的性骚扰。

13 日　美国广播公司新闻网站报道，美国新一届政府并没有释放关塔那摩监狱的任何囚犯，也没有公开任何获释人员或无罪人员的名单。

14 日　英国《独立报》网站报道，联合国人权理事会酷刑问题特别报告员尼尔斯·梅尔泽称在关塔那摩监狱的被拘禁者正在遭受国际法所禁止的酷刑和虐待，并敦促美国停止对关塔那摩监狱内被拘禁者施行酷刑。

14 日　美国有线电视新闻网报道，美国海军陆战队驻冲绳服役人员被指控殴打和强奸冲绳居民。

15 日　半岛电视台网站报道，2017 年 12 月 14 日，美国联邦通信委员会终止了 2015 年的《开放互联网规则》。这一做法废除了网络中立原则，允许互联网服务提供商可以有选择地对某些数据流进行阻塞或“节流”，这将加深富人与低收入群体之间的“数字鸿沟”。底特律“平衡互联网倡导”组织的纳西娅·瓦尔德兹认为，更昂贵的互联网将会对贫困人口更加不利，“这将是毁灭性的，会进一步加剧已经存在的不平等现象”。研究表明，94% 的招聘人员通过在线方式寻找求职者，更昂贵的互联网将会使美国的少数族裔和低收入人群的失业问题变得更糟。

15 日　据联合国人权高专办网站的报道，联合国人权理事会极端贫困和人权问题特别报告员菲利普·奥尔斯顿在对美国为期两周的实地考察后指出，“美国梦正在迅速蜕变为美国幻想”。他描述道：“我遇到很多人艰难地生存在洛杉矶贫民区，目睹了旧金山警官命令一群无家可归者离开，但对于他们能够去哪里却没有回答；我听说成千上万的穷人得到轻微违规通知书，它们似乎都是故意设计的，并很快演变成无法偿还的债务、监禁以及成为市政财政的补充；我看到很多州的污水处理场满负荷运行，那里的政府不认为卫生设施护理是他们的责任；我看见有人已经失去了全部牙齿，因为穷人享受的绝大多数医疗项目不包括成人牙科护理；我听说阿片类药物引起的死亡率飙升，并导致家庭、社区的破坏；我见到了生活在波多黎各煤灰山附近的人们，由于毫无保护措施，任由煤灰雨降在他们身上，带来疾病、残疾和死亡。”他指出，美国的财富、权力、技术都没有被用来解决 4000 万人持续贫困的局面。美国 25% 的青年生活在贫困中，其贫困率在经济合作与发展组织中是最高的，比该组织 14% 的平均贫困率高 11 个百分点。根据世界收入不平等数据库，美国是所有西方国家中基尼系数最高的国家，美国领导人正试图把这个国家变成“极端不平等的世界冠军”。他的结论是：“极端贫困的持续存在是当权者作出的政治选择。只要具有政治意愿，它就会迅速被消除。”

15 日　英国《卫报》网站报道，美国与同等发展水平国家之间的“健康差距”继续拉大。美国的人均医生和病床数比经济合作与发展组织国家平均水平少很多；与生活在其他富裕国家的人相比，美国人的预期寿命更短，更容易生病。包括寨卡病毒在内的热带疾病因未能得到应有重视而越来越常见。估计有1200万美国人生活在被忽视的寄生虫感染环境中。美国是发达国家中肥胖症患病率最高的国家；在获得水和公共卫生方面，美国名列世界第36位。

17日　半岛电视台网站报道，美国的“医疗荒漠”地带变得越来越普遍。自2010以来，超过80家乡村医院关闭，另有数百家医院濒临倒闭。

18日　《赫芬顿邮报》网站报道，联邦法官亚历克斯·科津斯基被至少15名女性指控对她们进行猥亵，发表不恰当的性评论，向她们展示色情内容。

18日　美国枪支暴力档案室发布的统计显示，截至12月18日，2017年美国共发生枪击事件60091起，其中大规模枪击事件338起；枪击事件共造成15182人死亡、30619人受伤，其中11岁以下儿童716人，12岁至17岁未成年人3178人。

27日　美国政治响应中心网站披露，截至12月27日，2017年利益集团在美国联邦层面的游说支出约为24.68亿美元，创近五年来新高。

31日　据《华盛顿邮报》网站统计，美国警察2017年共射杀987人。按照月份统计，美国警察2017年1月射杀92人，2月射杀100人，3月射杀76人，4月射杀67人，5月射杀74人，6月射杀84人，7月射杀94人，8月射杀82人，9月射杀70人，10月射杀85人，11月射杀84人，12月射杀79人。